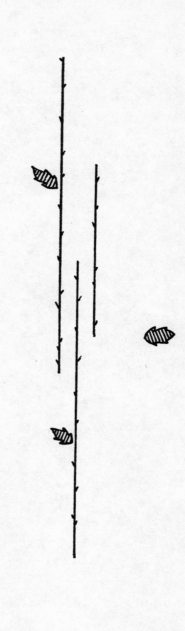

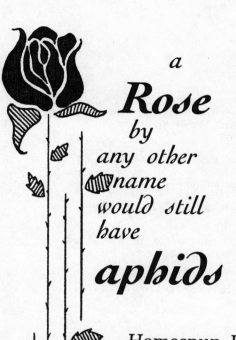

a
Rose
by
any other
name
would still
have

aphids

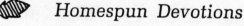

Homespun Devotions

Mab Graff Hoover

ZondervanPublishingHouse
Grand Rapids, Michigan
A Division of HarperCollinsPublishers

A Rose By Any Other Name Would Still Have Aphids
Copyright © 1992 by Mab Graff Hoover
All rights reserved

Requests for information should be addressed to:
Zondervan Publishing House
Grand Rapids, Michigan 49530

Library of Congress Cataloging-in-Publication Data

Hoover, Mab Graff
    A rose by any other name would still have aphids :
homespun devotions / Mab Graff Hoover
      p. cm.
    ISBN 0-310-54951-5 (pbk.)
      1. Meditations. 2. Hoover, Mab Graff. I. Title.
BV4832.2.H653 1991
242—dc20   91–44650
                                                            CIP

Edited by Mary McCormick
Cover design and illustration by Dennis Hill

Printed in the United States of America

92 93 94 95 96 97 / AK / 10 9 8 7 6 5 4 3 2 1

To my grandchildren —

Judi, Laurie, Danny, Timmy, Jenifer, David, Chrystal, Nicole, Kevin, and Melissa, and great grandson, Bryce. My prayer is that each of you will love our Lord Jesus Christ and serve Him.

Contents

A Note to the Reader

It's been a few years since I wrote *God Loves My Kitchen Best* and *God Still Loves My Kitchen*. These books were an account of my bumbling through life as a wife and mother. My kids are married now, have homes of their own, and as a result, many grandchildren have appeared. The last time I counted there were ten of them, ranging from wailing wigglers to ambling adolescents. Naturally, it has been my privilege to take care of them from time to time. Child care today has really changed since mine were little: I remember that I caused one of the babies to have a rash because I put the disposable diaper on wrong-side-out. I've never gotten used to the idea of carrying babies around in a hard plastic thing, either—and discipline is really different. When the kids get loud and unruly, it's definitely a no-no to yell, "Shut up!"

But, some things never change. Like my dear husband, Joe. You'd think that after sharing so many years together we would have all the rough edges sanded off our relationship. I'll admit I'm still a scatterbrain, but I'm *positive* I'm getting sweeter as the years go by, while *he's* as stubborn as ever.

My relationship with the Lord has changed, too. He seems more real to me now. I find myself talking to Him more—and He's always ready to help me out of a jam, even if it's my own fault. He cares about my everyday crises, such as not being able to find important papers at income tax time or forgetting to pay the bills. You probably don't do as many dumb things as I do, but whatever you do, whatever your problem is, He can help you, too.

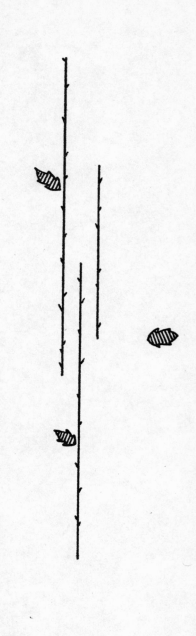

Happy New Year

Late Christmas afternoon after all the family had gone home, Joe told me that he was going to remodel the kitchen. "This will be the last Christmas you have to work in such a little space," he said, pointing toward the service porch with his toothpick. "Phase one will be to put the hot water heater outside."

I was glad and scared at the same time. Joe has done almost all the repair work on our home for years—but could he do plumbing and make cupboards? He didn't give me a chance to worry about it. The very next day he poured a concrete pad outside the back porch to put the water heater on.

New Year's morning he announced, "Instead of watching the parade, I'm going to move the heater outside."

I bit my lip. "Today? Maybe it would be better to wait and get a plumber."

"Plumber!" Brushing off the thought as though it were a pesky fly, he put on his old work jacket. "I'll have to turn off the water, but it won't take more than a couple of hours." He hitched up his pants, and started for the

13

garage to get his tools. Looking back, he flashed a confident smile. "Don't worry, Babe."

I put the breakfast dishes in the dishwasher along with some others. *Maybe I should start it while the water is still on,* I thought, but changed my mind when I remembered the water shortage. Joe was humming when he came back in carrying big wrenches and other destructive-looking tools.

In the living room I turned on the Tournament of Roses Parade and began to take ornaments off the tree. From the service porch I could hear grunting, pounding, scraping, grumbling, and an occasional, "What's wrong with this turkey?"

The parade was almost over when I realized how cold I was. I turned the furnace up to eighty degrees, but all I could hear was a click. "Joe!" I called, but he didn't answer. On the service porch the floor was wet and the back door wide open. Joe was outside, struggling to get the heater up on the pad. "Honey, the furnace won't come on," I said.

"I told you I had to turn the water off for a couple of hours," he said, frowning.

"What's that got to do with the furnace?" He pointed to the gas pipe on the tank. "Oh, yeah." I turned to go back in, saying, "Well, I'll make us some fresh coffee." Then I remembered. With the water turned off, I couldn't make coffee, get a drink, or even flush the toilet.

When the two hours were up, I heard no victorious cry, "It is finished!" Instead, Joe came into the living room, sat down in his chair, pulled off his shoes, and grinned one-sidedly. "I cut the pipes too short." He pulled an afghan over his legs and zipped up his jacket.

"But don't worry. I'll get more pipe first thing in the morning."

So, on New Year's day we ate at McDonald's, didn't get showers, the dishes didn't get washed, and we almost froze to death.

I came close to popping off with something ugly like, "I knew we should have called a plumber," but the Lord seemed to say to me, "Since when have you been perfect?"

> "Why do you look at the speck of sawdust in your brother's eye and pay no attention to the plank in your own eye?"
>
> Luke 6:41

It could have been worse. For one thing I hadn't invited all the family for New Year's dinner — and, thank goodness, the electric blanket still worked.

Love is patient, love is kind ... not easily angered, it keeps no record of wrongs.

1 Corinthians 13:4–5

Cupboards

"Was anybody hurt?" Don, my son-in-law, asked when he came into the kitchen. Joan and Don teach at a school nearby, and about every week or so we invite them and the grandkids for dinner.

I looked up from stirring spaghetti sauce. "What're you talking about?"

His blue eyes were innocent, and his face had an extra-serious expression, which is a dead giveaway that he's teasing me. He waved his hand around at the kitchen. All eleven doors and four drawers were open. "Just looks like a bomb exploded in there, so I wondered if anyone was hurt."

I threatened him with the wooden spoon. "I can't keep things neat when Joe's remodeling."

Joan giggled and hugged me. "Mother, you are the world's worst for leaving cupboard doors open. Don't you ever run into them?"

I gave her a look. "You should see the bruise on my hip from the breadboard."

She winked at Don. "As long as I can remember, Mother has left the cupboards open." No respect for her poor old mother.

"Hey, Grandad—" Now sixteen-year-old David was getting into it. "You'd do Grandmother a favor to take the doors off the cupboards."

Flustered, I banged shut a couple of doors. I decided right then that I would break myself of the open door policy. Before sitting down for dinner, I made a point of closing everything that was still open. All the family laughed at me. "Go ahead and laugh," I said. I lifted my chin. "You'll never catch me with my cupboards open again!"

The next day, I completely forgot about my vow until I cracked my shin on an open drawer in the bathroom. Moaning, and massaging my ankle, I slammed it shut. "That's it!" I shouted. "That's the last time!" But after grocery shopping, I even left the car door open when I went in the house, thinking, *What is the matter with me? Why can't I break the stupid habit?*

The next week, when I saw the family coming up the walk, I slammed the cupboard doors and drawers. Joan came to the kitchen, looked around and smiled. "Mother! I'm impressed. You really meant it last week." Her eyes were filled with admiration as she kissed my cheek. "I'll help you as soon as I wash my hands," she said and went toward the bathroom.

Oh, no. Oh, no! I had just showered, dried my hair, put on make-up, and used the curling iron—which meant she was going to see every cupboard door and drawer in the bathroom open.

The tongue is a small part of the body, but it makes great boasts.

James 3:5

17

I don't have victory over this bad habit yet, but I have realized that I need God's help even in the little, ridiculous, daily battles. Lord, help me become a door/drawer closer.

I can do everything through him who gives me strength.

Philippians 4:13

Chagrin

We're now into phase two of the kitchen remodeling—maybe it's phase three, because now I can't use either the washer or dryer. Joe is in the process of moving them where the trash compactor was, because he put *it* where the hot water tank used to be. That's okay. It gives me a truthful excuse not to wash clothes. The only bad thing about this phase is that he had to take the cupboards down above the washer and dryer, and all the stuff I kept in them is now lined up around the walls on the kitchen floor. "This state of chaos will last for an indefinite time," he said, "because I have to take time out to work on the car."

I hope no one drops in for a meal until I can put this cleaning stuff away. The smell of food cooking, combined with the odors of Sani-Flush, Lysol, Fantastic, Simple Green, bleach, and soap is not too appetizing. I've already been embarrassed about how messy it looks. The day Joe pulled the washing machine and dryer out from the wall to work on the cupboards, our neighbor across the street dropped in. She's the one whose house and yard look like something out of *Good Housekeeping*, and

19

the one whom, I keep thinking, I ought to invite to church.

It was awful. I was in dirty sweats—the red ones that have a bleached spot right on the stomach—and I was dirty because I was putting away Christmas stuff in the garage. She came walking up the driveway in her designer jeans and smelling like Halston.

"I noticed you moved your hot water tank outside," she said, coming right up the back steps, "and I was wondering if I could see what you're doing?" Dying inwardly, I tried to smile as I invited her in. Do you have any idea how much yukky dirt lurks beneath your washing machine and dryer? Lint-covered socks—a moldy cookie—a fuzzy spoon—peanuts. She walked right through it and wanted to know what we planned to do in the kitchen. I could barely mumble something about phases one through four, much less invite her to church.

Rats. I was waiting for just the right time to be a good witness to her. I wanted the house to be clean and to have my make-up on and be wearing something cute . . . But the Lord seemed to bring this thought to mind . . . *I can use you any time, in any circumstances—if you are willing.*

Preach the Word; be prepared in season and out of season.

2 Timothy 4:2

20

I will *invite her over for coffee, and we'll talk about church* ... *even before the kitchen is finished.*

Always be prepared to give an answer to everyone who asks you to give the reason for the hope that you have.

1 Peter 3:15

Grocery Gremlins

Do you think it's possible for very small gremlins to be hiding in the shelves at the supermarkets? When I put away the groceries today, I discovered I had bought a box of Puffed *Rice* instead of Puffed Wheat. I hate Puffed Rice and would never have chosen that box. I know I can take it back, but it's so irritating to be outsmarted by something one can't see. "I *know* I picked up a box of Puffed Wheat," I complained to Joan, but she raised an eyebrow and looked at Don, and his lip twitched as he tried to keep from smiling. "It's true!" I stamped my foot. "And last week I put a can of cream of mushroom soup in the basket, but when I got home it was cream of celery!" They laughed out loud.

"How about the chocolate chip cookies that turned into oatmeal cookies?" Joe teased.

I know they're making fun of me, but when I reach for a certain item I *know* I'm in the right spot, and somehow, between the shelf and my basket *somebody* makes a switch. I read labels very carefully, especially now that I'm trying to watch our salt and fat intake, so how could this happen? I'm sure some kind of intelligent

22

life lurks behind the groceries and with a twisted mind moves items around just as I reach for them.

Even worse, I think those gremlins come home with me, then hide valuable papers, misplace my glasses, and erase important calendar dates.

Still, in my heart I know that these goofs are my own fault. I'm just trying to make excuses for my absentmindedness—just like when I blame the Devil for my sins.

> Each one is tempted when, by his own evil desire, he is dragged away and enticed.
>
> James 1:14

Guess what else I found in the groceries? A package of doughnuts! Honestly, I hardly ever buy doughnuts. Either someone else is absentminded, or there are gremlins.

> The heart is deceitful above all things and beyond cure. Who can understand it?
>
> Jeremiah 17:9

Playing Games

Bob, Bonnie, and their five-year-old, Kevin, our kids who live up north, were here for the weekend. We were really glad to see them even though the kitchen still looks like an unloading dock. We had planned to go to Knott's Berry Farm on Saturday, but it rained all day. All-day rain on Sunday forced us to think of ways to keep from getting cabin fever. We watched television, worked on handcrafts, got caught up on the family news, then started playing games.

While playing Scrabble with Bonnie, I heard Bob say, "No, Kevin, Daddy doesn't want to play that game with you."

Later, I heard Joe say, "Nope. Grandad's not going to play that with you again. You always beat."

"You guys!" I admonished. "How can you be so cruel to a five-year-old who's stuck in the house with four adults!" I smiled at Kevin. "*Grandmother* will play with you, Honey!"

Kevin pursed his lips and eyed me critically. "I'll probably win," he prophesied. He brought a colored plastic frame over and placed it between us.

"What do I do?" I asked, as he divided colored discs.
"We drop our pieces in these columns." He smiled
slyly. "We have to block each other from getting a row."
I raised my eyebrows. "That's it? Piece of cake."
"I'll start," he said generously and plinked his piece
in a slot.
"Hah!" I said and plunked my piece on top of it.
Silently he dropped another alongside, and just as
silently I blocked it. *Plink, plunk, plink, plunk.* The slots
began to fill up. *What's so hard about this,* I wondered.
Suddenly, he looked up at me, grinning. "Gotcha!"
Sure enough, he had a perfect row. How had it
happened? I thought I had blocked him every time.
"Okay, okay," I barked. I could feel my face getting hot.
"Let's try it again."
Three times we played that dumb game, and three
times he beat me.
"Want to try again?" he asked, smirking.
I looked at Bob and Joe, both grinning like Cheshire
cats. I scowled at them. "No I do not. You're too good for
me."
There must be some lesson here. It's humbling to be
outsmarted three times in a row by a five-year-old.

Do not think of yourself more highly than you
ought.

Romans 12:3

*(Between you and me, I felt a lot better later on when I beat
Kevin at Parcheesi.)*

"Therefore, whoever humbles himself like this
child is the greatest in the kingdom of heaven."

Matthew 18:4

25

Garbage Disposal

Phase four of the project is coming along nicely—I haven't been able to use the sink for two days, but I'm so excited! I have a new, almond-colored sink. My old sink was stained and chipped, and no amount of scrubbing made it shine, so yesterday Joe said, "I think it's time you had a new one." It took him about two minutes to disconnect the old one and toss it out.

To save money, we decided to buy the new sink at Home Depot, which is about ten miles away. When we got home, we discovered that we'd bought the wrong size flex tubing to hook it up, so in evening traffic, facing the setting sun, we drove back and exchanged it. No matter what we buy, our standard procedure is: (1) Buy it; (2) discover it's wrong; (3) have a panic attack looking for sales slip; (4) return it for exchange.

Too tired last night to finish the job, Joe was all set this morning to hook up the sink. "Hey, Babe!" he yelled. "Would you mind holding the garbage disposal up here in place while I prop it underneath with this two-by-four?"

I came running from the bedroom and looked at the

gaping hole where the sink had been. "We have to hook up the disposal before I can put in the new sink," he explained.

The only way I could get a good grip on that heavy thing was to climb up on the counter, partly straddle the opening, kneel, then reach down and grab it with both hands. Joe was on his back, directly underneath, trying to push the board under the disposal. "This piece is a tad too long." He wriggled out and stood up. "I'll have to saw it off. Won't take a minute. Can you hold it?"

While I held that heavy, fat, blue thing in place, my mind was racing. I thought of all the garbage it had disposed of for me. I remembered an angel food cake that had looked beautiful when I took it out of the oven but by the time it cooled was only an inch high and tougher than cardboard. Blue Boy had gobbled down that mistake in a hurry. When I've allowed it to do its work, it has kept me from gaining weight, too. Many times I've been tempted to eat the last spoonful of gravy, or the last sliver of pie, but impulsively tossed it to the "eliminator" instead. Good old Blue Boy. If I could keep only one of the kitchen appliances, I would choose the garbage disposal.

Up on the counter, hunched over, my hips, legs and arms aching as I waited for Joe to come back, I made a spiritual comparison. How much garbage has the Lord disposed of for me? When He gave up his life to die on the cross as a sacrifice for sins, He disposed of all my sins—pride, disobedience, fears, jealousies, hate—and every bad thing I ever did. He continues to get rid of the evil things in my life, as long as I bring them to Him.

Joe has the sink hooked up now, including the

disposal, and everything works perfectly. He says we're ready for phase five now—refinishing the cupboards.

"Come now, let us reason together," says the Lord. "Though your sins are like scarlet, they shall be as white as snow; though they are red as crimson, they shall be like wool."

Isaiah 1:18

When I told Joe's mom and sister about the new sink, they bragged about him, which is no more than right. He had done a great job. But I thought he should have mentioned the fact that I perched up on the counter, in great pain, for at least five minutes.

"For everything in the world—the cravings of sinful man—the lust of his eyes and the boasting of what he has and does—comes not from the Father but from the world.

1 John 2:16

"If we confess our sins, he . . . will forgive us.

1 John 1:9

28

TV Movies

One Sunday our pastor said, "People don't have to agree about everything in order to be friends." I'm glad he said that, because I know that Joe and I are friends—but we sure don't agree about TV movies. He can sit down and watch two minutes of any movie and be hooked on it. No matter how far-fetched or corny it is, he can watch it to the stupid end. And, he never gets sleepy. Television is a narcotic for me. Fifteen minutes into any show and I'm asleep. A story has to be plausible, romantic, hilarious, scary, and heart-wrenching to keep me awake. I spend almost every evening catnapping from eight until ten. For some reason, it distresses Joe for me to doze off during a movie, so I try hard to keep him from knowing it. So that my head doesn't loll over, I sit up straight, brace my head against a cushion, and struggle to keep my eyes open. I try to make appropriate answers to his remarks and to chuckle a little when he laughs. I usually wake up when the program is almost over, when cars are sailing off mountain roads, sirens are wailing, and women are screaming. With all the excitement, I begin to get a little interested. Last night, for example,

29

when I came to, I asked "Why is that white car turning around?" The first time I asked, Joe was so engrossed he didn't hear, but the second time he looked at me, bug-eyed. "Why? Good grief! Don't you remember what the driver of the other car *said*?"

I tried desperately to pick up the story without letting him know that I'd been out of it for at least an hour. By this time the goofball in the white car skidded to a stop, leaped out, and raced across a field. "Is he going to rescue the blonde?"

As soon as I asked that question, Joe pounced on me. "Aha! You were asleep, weren't you?" While the credits were still running, he snapped off the set. "Boy, you missed a really good picture."

Television is here to stay, and even though Joe and I don't agree on what to watch, we are still the best of friends. I bring him coffee in the mornings, and he rubs my neck and shoulders at night. I write all the checks and balance the checkbook (sort of), and he is still working hard at making my kitchen beautiful.

A friend loves at all times.

Proverbs 17:17

As iron sharpens iron, so one [friend] sharpens another.

Proverbs 27:17

Yes, Joe is definitely my friend, but I think we should watch more shows that I like. Then maybe he'd be the one who snoozes.

[Jesus said] "I no longer call you servants ... I have called you friends."

John 15:15

Red Dress

"The Valentine party at church is next Saturday night," I said. "I don't have anything to wear."

"Well—" Joe sighed. "I guess we'll have to go shopping."

"We can't afford it. Since Christmas, and all the new stuff we've had to buy for the kitchen—"

He shrugged, meaning it was my problem. He installed sinks, fixed pipes, made repairs, and took care of the car. The housework, check writing, food, and clothes were my department. I knew that if I said too much about not having anything to wear he'd suggest we stay home. I really didn't have anything to wear—at least, nothing I hadn't worn to church over and over and over. I wanted something special for this party. Discouraged, I went to the bedroom, and although I had already searched the closet, I began to sort through my clothes again. I sighed. Nothing. Then I saw it. An old plastic garment bag I had kept in the back of the closet, wherever we moved, for at least thirty years. I knew what was in it. A red crepe de chine *silk* dress, with a V neck, trimmed with two rows of long red fringe. Years ago, before I knew

Christ, I had bought that dress for a New Year's Eve party. After I accepted Jesus, the dress didn't fit my lifestyle, but I had hung on to it. It was so beautiful and so expensive, I just couldn't give it up.

Slowly, I took it out of the bag and walked over to the window to inspect it. It hadn't faded a bit.

Excited, I took off my blouse and jeans. *If only I can get in it!* I pulled on the lovely thing and zipped it up. Although it was too snug across my hips and stomach, I could still wear it! I flipped back and forth in front of the mirror and watched the fringe swish around my hips. I grinned at myself. "Valentine party, here I come!"

The night of the dinner I fiddled with my hair and make-up quite a while before putting on the red dress. Joe was already in his suit and watching TV when I bounced in and stood before him, smiling flirtatiously. But he didn't say any of the usual complimentary things. He stared at me with his mouth sort of twisted. He rubbed his chin, and still didn't say anything. I frowned at him. "Don't you like it?"

"Do you like it?" he countered.

Part of a Scripture verse popped into my mind: *Put off your old self . . .*

In the mirror over the piano I looked at my image. The Holy Spirit repeated, *Put off your old self.* My old self. How well I remembered that person. Self-centered, willful, show-off, always out for a good time. I suddenly felt deflated. I turned my back to him. "Unzip me, please."

I stepped out of the red dress and held it up. We'd had many hilarious nights together. It just wouldn't be true to say I hadn't had fun wearing it. But Paul said, "I consider everything a loss compared to the surpassing greatness of knowing Christ Jesus my Lord" (Philippians 3:8). Did any of the good times in the old life compare with the joy I have in my new life? No! My sins all forgiven, a purpose for living, a Christian husband. I leaned over and kissed him. "This dress is too tight anyway. I'll put on my blue dress."

He let out his breath and grinned. "You always look nice in that."

As I headed for the bedroom, I called over my shoulder. "I'm going to get rid of this dress!"

"What are you going to do with it?"

I grinned at him. "Give it to the missionaries!"

You were taught, with regard to your former way of life, to put off your old self ... be made new in the attitude of your minds ... put on the new self, created to be like God.

Ephesians 4:22–24

(I wonder, though, if I could let the seams out a little? Or maybe make a blouse out of it?)

Do not conform any longer to the pattern of this world, but be transformed by the renewing of your mind.... Rather, clothe yourselves with the Lord Jesus Christ.

Romans 12:2; 13:14

Nix on Pix

We didn't especially want our pictures taken, but all the kids kept saying they didn't have any recent photos of us, so we finally made an appointment at our neighborhood photography studio.

On the day we went, the waiting room was packed with anxious mothers, fretful babies, and bored teenagers. We almost turned around and left, but an hour later an exhausted photographer invited us into her studio. She gave Joe a tired smile. "Sir, if you'll just sit on this bench, facing the camera, and you, dear—" she touched my arm— "straddle the bench, just like you're on a horse, and press your chest against his shoulder." She must have taken thirty pictures, telling us to smile, look this way, look over there, and let's have a *big* smile. By the time she was through taking pictures, my hip joints felt like I'd actually been on a horse.

A week later they called us in to look at the proofs. "I'm amazed," I said. "These are really good."

Looking over my shoulder, Joe grinned. "Flattering, you mean." He nudged me with his elbow. "Our wrinkles don't look so deep."

The desk clerk was smiling, too. "They really are good. If I were you, I'd order at least three eight-by-tens, and—"

"Oh, no!" I exclaimed. "We'd never use that many. We'll take one eight-by-ten for ourselves, and four five-by-sevens for our children."

She frowned. "I'm sorry, Mrs. Hoover, but you can't do that. You have to order at least two eight-by-tens, eight five-by-sevens, and twenty-four wallet size."

Of course we paid the bill—almost a hundred dollars.

"I don't know what we'll do with all these pictures," I said the next week when we picked up the huge brown envelope.

At home I tossed it on the kitchen table, intending to look at the pictures that evening, but a week later, when Joan and Don came for dinner, the envelope had disappeared.

"You must have done something with it," Joe accused. "Did you file it?"

I bit my lip. The truth was: I couldn't remember. We looked through the files, in every drawer, the magazine rack, all the closets, and the refrigerator—but that envelope was gone. "Oh, why didn't I put it away instead of leaving it on the table?" I moaned.

"You must have tossed it, Mother," Joan said. "Remember the time you threw away the gift certificate for the Velvet Turtle?"

Joe shook his head. "It was for thirty-five dollars, too."

I felt so sad and senile. How could I have been so careless?

Two months later, Joe and I were having coffee at the

kitchen table, sorting out the day's trash mail. He looked out across the yard and chewed on his toothpick. "You know, Babe, I think I must have thrown those pictures out with the trash the next day. I vaguely remember seeing a brown envelope and thinking, *She doesn't need to save this old envelope.* He looked at me, his blue eyes troubled. "You know how you're always saving old envelopes?"

I stared at him with my mouth open. I didn't know whether to bop him or kiss him. Two months of worry and regret. But it was *his* fault! And I wasn't senile after all!

> "For hardship does not spring from the soil, nor does trouble sprout from the ground. Yet man is born to trouble as surely as sparks fly upward."
> Job 5:6–7

I admit I should have put away the pictures in the first place, but it sure made me feel better for Joe to "fess up."

Confess your sins to each other.

James 5:16

When the Cat's Away

Because our preacher son, Ron, and his wife, Barbara, live about fifty-five miles south of us in Laguna Hills, we don't get to see them and their three kids as often as we'd like. Barbara sells "Home Interiors" merchandise, so I was glad to attend one of her parties. The day of the party, I worried a little bit about leaving Joe. I knew that I'd be gone at least five hours, and I never know what *project* he'll start when he's lonely. A few years ago he casually mentioned that he'd like to build a patio sometime, and when I came back from the store he had already chopped away part of the back sidewalk.

When I came home from Barbara's, I punched the garage door-opener, but when the door opened there was no room to drive in. All the kitchen cupboard doors and the drawers were laid out on the floor, and Joe was on his knees with the sander going full blast. He stopped and slowly stood up, rubbing his back.

I got out of the car and kissed his dusty cheek. "My goodness! What are you doing?"

"I decided to refinish the cupboards today." His eyes sparkled with enthusiasm. "Have to sand everything down to the bare wood." He held one old dark cupboard door next to a sanded one.

"Oh, Honey! The wood is beautiful!" I was smiling when I went into the kitchen.

"What do you think?" he asked.

I stood in the doorway and looked around. I could feel my mouth open. Those cupboard doors outside—the dishes, glasses, canned goods, pots and pans—everything was exposed for the whole world to see the clutter. Black, gaping holes where drawers had been, seemed like mouths howling in pain. (Later I found that their contents had been dumped carefully in piles in our bedroom.) Even my secret junk cupboard had been uncovered, revealing cracked vases, a piece of red cellophane I'd saved for years, heart-shaped boxes, Easter baskets stuffed with faded green grass, and old mayonnaise jars. Everything—table, counters, toaster, dishes, stove top—was covered with a layer of varnish dust. Even the linoleum had footprints all over it.

"Sorry about the dust, Babe. I took everything I could out to the garage, but I had to sand the sides and framework in here."

Why hadn't he sanded *before* he took the doors off? Or at least draped some towels over the stuff? Now I'd have to do all the dishes, dust everything, mop. How could he have made such a mess in one day? I shouldn't have left him alone. I should have stayed home and protected things.

Barbara has invited me to another party, but I'm not going. I don't dare leave home until he gets this kitchen project finished.

A wife of noble character who can find? . . . She
watches over the affairs of her household.

Proverbs 31:10, 27

*I guess I should be thankful he didn't knock out a wall while
I was gone.*

Be on your guard; stand firm in the faith.

1 Corinthians 16:13

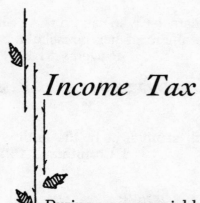

Income Tax

During a commercial last night Joe reminded me that it was time to start getting the income tax stuff together.

"Phooey," I groaned, leaning back against the couch. "How I dread this time of year!"

"I don't like paying taxes any more than you do, but we have to."

"Paying taxes isn't what I meant. It's trying to find all the papers." He raised an eyebrow and I knew what he was thinking. "You don't believe I have a system, do you?" I yelped. "After all the years of child rearing, housekeeping, and all the office jobs I've had, don't you think I know we must have a place for everything and everything in its place?"

"Hey! Did I say anything? I know you have everything filed. So all you have to do is dig out the records and we'll get them up to Les."

"But you just watch, some important paper will be missing. Like last year. Remember that two hundred and some dollars your company reported to the IRS as interest earned on some profit-sharing thing?"

"Yeah, and we were penalized for it."

"I *know* we didn't get any notice of it."

His eyebrow went up again. "Big companies don't make mistakes like that. You must have thrown it out. Like that gift certificate to the Velvet Turtle."

"The Velvet Turtle! You always bring that up." I jumped up with hands on hips. "*You* were the one who threw out the photos!"

He nodded. "I know. I said I was sorry."

But I wasn't ready to quit yipping. I could tell him about a few other things he'd misplaced—like the whole garage. I started toward the kitchen, and unexpectedly, through Scripture, the Holy Spirit whispered: *Blessed are the peacemakers.*

I struggled with the Spirit a moment or two before I calmed down. I poured coffee and brought him a cup. "Well, Honey, let's not argue. But things certainly do have a way of disappearing around here." I sat on his chair arm and hugged him. "I don't remember ever seeing that notice from the company last year." I sighed. "You're probably right, though. I might have thrown it out with the junk mail. Only the Lord knows what important things I've thrown out this year."

Alone in the bathroom, I thanked the Lord for closing my mouth before I said anything else. I always bluster the loudest when I feel guilty. I know it's my responsibility to take care of our records. Joe trusts me completely. If I were in charge of the books at some company, would I be more careful?

Whatever you do, work at it with all your heart,
as working for the Lord, not for men.

Colossians 3:23

41

Another thing I could have reminded him of — last week he left the garage open all night.

Don't have anything to do with foolish and stupid arguments, because you know they produce quarrels.

2 Timothy 2:23

Tissue Overlooked

I'm not a natural-born "washer and ironer." In fact, I hate those chores. When they finally invented something as wonderful as no-iron material, why would the fashion experts put us all back in wrinkled cotton? Oh, well. That's not what I'm disgusted about. Today I'm just wondering if other women have as much trouble as I do on wash day with stuff left in the pockets.

I know how to do a washing. Sorting clothes is one of the earliest things my mother taught me—three piles: white, colored, and dark. I also learned at an early age to turn pockets wrong side out. I've picked up quite a bit of change doing that, but I've also missed a coin now and then, which makes a nerve-wracking clank-clank-clank with each twist of the agitator. Yet, the thing that makes me really grouchy—and in spite of my experience, it happens over and over—is an innocent piece of Kleenex, tucked in somebody's pocket.

Is anything more exasperating than to open the washer after it has shut off, and discover fuzzy lint on everything? Makes me want to throw the whole load in the trash. How can one Kleenex make every garment look

43

like an Angora sweater? I remember a black cotton T-shirt that was absolutely ruined by a stowaway Kleenex. I picked at those stubborn pieces of lint for days before I finally gave up and put it in the Goodwill bag.

It happened to me again this morning. This time the tissue must have been hiding in the sleeve of a sweatshirt that I washed along with my best wine-colored bath towels. When I opened the washer, anger popped out all over me like a bad case of measles. Although I've already rewashed them, my towels still look as though they're covered with snow.

What really infuriates me is that I have no one to blame but myself. When the kids were home, I could get on them for leaving stuff in their pockets, but I can't blame Joe. He uses handkerchiefs.

Well—I'd better get over this "mad" or the results will be worse than fuzz on everything. The last time I was this put out, I got Joe all upset, and then he barked at his mom and threw his shoe at our cat, Samson. Anger spreads worse than lint.

Do not be quickly provoked in your spirit, for anger resides in the lap of fools.
Ecclesiastes 7:9

I wonder if Joe could invent a detection device, like the metal detectors at the airport, that could detect Kleenex?

Everyone should be quick to listen, slow to speak and slow to become angry.
James 1:19

Hoover's Law

Murphy's Law: Anything that can possibly go wrong will go wrong, and will do so at the worst possible time.

Yesterday I'd cleaned house until it sparkled because the deacon board was meeting at our house. Joe asked me a couple of times if there was anything he could do to help, but I said, "No, I'll take care of everything inside, and you take care of your stuff." Meaning, the yards, garage, watering—and stay out of my way. I don't know what he did all day because I was too busy cleaning and baking Mrs. Smith's frozen pies. About four o'clock I was ready for company, and he came in ready for something to eat.

"We can't eat now," I said, waving at the cups, glasses, plates, and napkins artistically arranged on the table. "We'll have refreshments later." He picked up a banana, tossed the peeling into the shining sink, went into the living room, and took a handful of assorted nuts from the cut-glass bowl on the coffee table.

"Hey!" I followed him in. "Those are for tonight!" I snatched the dish and put it on top of the television.

"That reminds me—the bulb in this lamp is burned out." As I unscrewed it, I looked around the room. "I wish we had better light in here. Only the people who sit by the lamps will be able to see their notes."

He snapped his fingers, jumped up, and hustled out the back door. In a few moments he came back with a huge, dusty, brass chandelier that used to be in the kitchen. He held it up toward the ceiling. "All I have to do is get up in the attic, bring a wire, and drill—"

"Not now!" I slumped in a chair as I visualized acoustic litter all over the carpet. "I just meant sometime, maybe before we have another meeting here." I opened the front door for the late afternoon breeze and looked at the lawn. "Oh. You decided not to mow?"

"Wow, that's right!" Before I could stop him, he dashed out and started the mower.

While he was charging around the yard behind the mower, I took the chandelier out to the garage, then checked through the house to see if I'd overlooked anything disgusting. In the front bathroom I about had a heart attack. He had already smeared up the soap! He had used a guest towel! His footprints were on the shag rug! I got rid of the evidence quickly, then stepped out to see how he was doing.

He had finished mowing and was sprinkling the lawn when the deacons began to arrive. Wet grass clippings were on the sidewalk and porch. In fact, little green blades were everywhere. During the meeting I noticed one man picking bits of grass off his pants and shoes. When I served the pie, there was even a piece of grass on one of my hands.

After everyone went home, I asked my husband why

he had mowed the lawn so late in the afternoon. "You didn't even have time for a shower."

He looked puzzled and hurt. "You said you wanted the lawn to look nice for tonight."

How can I find fault with a man whose timing is just a little off?

> There is a time for everything and a season for every activity . . . a time to tear down and a time to build.
>
> Ecclesiastes 3:1, 3

I think Joe has his own Murphy's Law — "When it's almost time for company to arrive, get chores done."

> Be very careful, then, how you live—not as unwise but as wise, making the most of every opportunity.
>
> Ephesians 5:15, 16

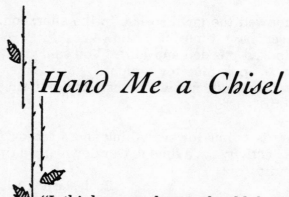

Hand Me a Chisel

"I think every home should be equipped with special tools for opening today's processed foods," I grumbled as I pulled and twisted a tab on a can of cat food. Joe was in the kitchen, his tools spread out on both counters, and Samson and Josephine were "me-ow-me-owing" with every breath.

"Here, I'll do it," Joe said. With ease he zipped off the top and handed the can to me.

"You're stronger than I am." I put some of the stinky food in two pet bowls and put them on the floor. "I still think we should have tools to open stuff. Milk cartons, for example—they must seal the tops with Crazy Glue."

Joe tightened the last hinge on a cupboard door, then smiled at me as one smiles at a half-wit. He rubbed the newly varnished wood lovingly. "Looks pretty good, huh?"

"Looks wonderful, Honey." At last! One of the cupboards had a door on it. I took a carton of milk from the refrigerator. "But going back to how hard things are to open, now look at this. It says, 'Push Up Here,' see? Okay. I'm pushing up, but the dumb thing won't open."

He sighed and took the carton. "I never knew anyone to have so much trouble opening things." He pulled at the carton, but it stayed tightly sealed.

I let out an exultant snicker. "I told you! Here's the paring knife. Just keep poking at it until it's open. That's what I do."

He carefully worked the spout open. "You poke it with a knife? No wonder the milk spurted all over the counter last night."

I stumbled over Sam on my way to the pantry and reached for a cereal box. "How about these boxes that say, 'Press here for *easy* opening?'" I held up a box that looked as though it had been damaged in handling. "I've pressed until the box caved in, but those dotted lines are still closed."

He put the milk back in the refrigerator. "Honey, your problem is that you're too impatient."

"Maybe so." I stepped over Josephine. "But when the package says: 'EASY OPEN'—I know I'm in for a struggle."

"Poor girl."

I shrugged off his hug. He just didn't understand what the average homemaker has to go through. "And once the cereal package is open, the inner liner is another hassle. And all those seasoning mixes that say 'Tear Here'—I break more nails that way."

He shook his head and walked into the front room. "I still say you're in too much of a hurry, Babe."

Maybe he's right, but that doesn't change the fact that stuff is hard to open. This morning I tried to open a big box of detergent with directions to "Pull string here." Could I pull it? Not until I tackled it with a pair of pliers. Then there're frozen food packages, meat, and bakery goods sealed in plastic, and bath soap locked eternally in cardboard. I don't intend to tell Joe, but sometimes I have bitten packages open. That's why I need tools designed to open this stuff. (So I won't ruin my teeth.)

> The end of a matter is better than its beginning, and patience is better than pride.
>
> Ecclesiastes 7:8

Maybe I can exercise my patience by waiting for Joe to open all the cat food, milk, cereal, and frozen food. Hee, hee, hee.

Be joyful in hope, patient in affliction, faithful in prayer.

Romans 12:12

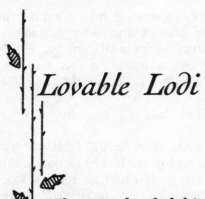

Lovable Lodi

"Where you headed this time?" my neighbor, Larita, asked as she watched me put stuff in our RV.

"To visit Dena and Johnny—you know, my sis? They live in Lodi."

"Where's that?"

"About four hundred miles north of Los Angeles."

"Wow, that's a long way."

"Yep. About eight hours." I put a box of groceries inside the Southwind's door. "We usually go up twice a year—always in February or March. Dena's son-in-law is a CPA and he does our income tax."

"With gas so high why don't you take your car instead of the RV?"

I looked up at the huge vehicle. "I think Joe likes to drive it. And, Dena doesn't have room for us to stay all night. Anyway, it's pretty nice to have our own bedroom, bath, and TV—especially since Johnny likes 'Wheel of Fortune' and 'Jeopardy,' and Joe likes 'Inside Edition' and 'A Current Affair'!"

"Oh, oh." She looked at me wisely. "Sounds like you have a problem. Do they ever get really mad at each other?"

"Nah. I think they're even fond of each other."

"You hope!" She waved and went home.

Joe came out with more stuff to go. He looked grumpy. "Man, you take a lot for a few days."

I frowned. "You don't want to go, do you? We don't have to . . ."

"Yeah we do. Les has all our tax stuff in his computer."

"We should get a tax man here." I bit my lip. "But you know it's an excuse for me to see Dena." I followed him into the RV. "I know you just go for my sake." He didn't deny it. "I know it's a long drive." Silence.

Dejected and feeling guilty, I went back in the house. I felt selfish. I decided to call off the trip.

But then I heard Joe whistling! I smiled. Joe only whistles when he's *happy!*

So Abram said to Lot, "Let's not have any quarreling between you and me . . . for we are brothers."

Genesis 13:8

Joe came in the house, grinning. "Don't worry, Honey. You and I always have a good time together." He gave me a quick kiss. "Maybe I'll even watch 'Wheel of Fortune.'"

If we walk in the light, as he is in the light, we have fellowship with one another.

1 John 1:7

En Route

"Yippee! We're on our way!" I buckled the seat belt and looked at the traffic on the San Bernardino freeway. "Isn't it fun to be 'way up high' like we're in a truck?"

"We *are* in a truck." Joe suddenly hit the brakes and our lane halted. "Sure wish we could have left an hour earlier. Morning traffic is the pits."

"It's hard to get away. I had to water the plants, and feed the cats and ..." Traffic began to move again. "Honey, don't you just love our RV?" I turned and looked back at the little sink, stove, and table. "So cute!" I took a deep breath. "Do you smell anything?"

"Nothing but the diesel ahead of us."

"No, no. Smells like propane."

"You couldn't be smelling propane. Everything's turned off."

"Are you sure? How about the refrigerator? I *smell* it!"

He signaled, then pulled over and stopped. After checking all around, he waited for a chance to move back into traffic.

On our way up the Grapevine, a long steep hill between the San Fernando Valley and Bakersfield, I gasped, then yelled, "What was *that*?"

Joe looked terrified. "What was what?!"

"Don't you hear that thump-thumping?"

Joe cocked his head. "I don't hear anything. Wish you wouldn't scare me."

"I can't understand why you can't hear that thumping."

"Well, go look around. I'd like a snack while you're up, anyway."

I couldn't find anything wrong, but when I opened the refrigerator I let out a moan.

"What now?" Joe was looking at me in the rearview mirror.

"I'm sure the fridge is defrosting."

"Look in the freezer. Do you still have ice cubes?"

"Yeah—but—"

"If you're going to worry the whole trip—"

"I'm not *worried*! I'm just trying to watch out for any emergency. Is the engine getting hot?"

He looked at the gauge. "No, Babe."

I brought him a couple of cookies and poured coffee. I sat down and tried to relax. After a while I said, "I wonder if there'll be any wind farther up? Remember the time I-5 was closed because of wind?"

"I can drive in the wind. Quit worrying."

I took a vow of silence. Man! I never knew anybody who was so quick to misunderstand!

"Know what?" I asked two minutes later. "I think I left the iron on."

Joe sucked in his breath. "You gotta be kidding!"

"Well, I'm not for sure positive, but, remember last night I was pressing those things?"

"You took the ironing board down, remember?"

"Oh, yeah. Whew." I took a sip of coffee. "Hope Kim takes good care of the cats."

"She will." He smiled wryly. "For eight years they've escaped death."

As we neared Stockton, I yowled, "Joe! I *know* I smell something burning! Maybe the brake fluid is gone, or the transmission fluid, or—"

"All you're smelling is other trucks. Trust me. Do you want to get to your sister's today? Then quit worrying and let me drive."

What a grouch!

If you make the Most High your dwelling—even the Lord, who is my refuge—then no harm will befall you, no disaster will come near.

Psalm 91:9–10

Safe in Lodi! Now all I have to worry about is the trip home.

Jesus said ". . . do not worry about your life. . . . Consider the ravens: . . . God feeds them. And how much more valuable you are than birds! Who of you by worrying can add a single hour to his life?"

Luke 12:22, 24–25

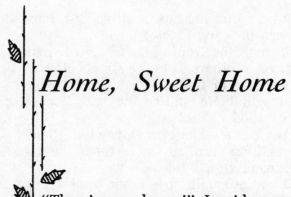

Home, Sweet Home

"There's our house!" I said as we came around the curve. "The old saying, 'There's no place like home' is certainly true, isn't it?"

"Yep." Joe pushed his cap back. "I'm glad to be home."

"We did have a good time, though, don't you think?"

He smiled. "Yeah. We really did. I enjoyed seeing all the family at Shirley's, and Sis cooked some good meals." He stopped in front of our house. "The grass sure needs watering." He began to back our twenty-seven foot RV into the driveway. "Flowers look dead."

"I thought Kim was going to water. Hope Sam and Josephine are okay."

When we got out and walked across the patio, both cats were asleep and not the least interested in us. "So much for a royal welcome."

Joe opened the back door and groaned. "Ants have taken over."

Before we could do anything else, we had to clean up ants. When we had finally sprayed and wiped and washed away every one, we sat down and opened the mail.

"Bills!" Joe groused. "Nothing but bills."

"And junk."

"This telephone bill! Who lives in Bellflower you called?"

"*I* called?" I snatched the bill from him and stared at it. "*You* must have called."

"No, Mab. I did not."

"Joe, you must have called when you were trying to find parts for something." The old goof. He couldn't remember whom he had called.

"Didn't you call Charlotte?"

I bit my lip. "Oh, yeah."

Listening to the answering machine, I could see a thin layer of dust on the desk. More housecleaning. The machine reported that our son Ron was sick and seeing a doctor, the March of Dimes wanted me to collect for them, and we had missed seeing dear friends who were in the area for one night.

Joe stretched, then hunched his shoulders. "Well, I guess we better get to unloading."

Passing him in the driveway with my arms full of clothes, I called over my shoulder, "Not as fun unloading as loading."

"You got that right. Maybe we should become full-timers and never go home."

I thought about Peter when he had that wonderful time up on the Mount of Transfiguration. He had an experience of joy far above anything I've ever known on any trip. Yet, when he came down the mountain, it was just an ordinary day, and the tax collectors were on his case about Jesus' not paying temple tax. In order to pay, he had to forget seeing Jesus glorified, put on smelly old clothes, get his fishing pole out, dig some bait, and get to work.

> [Jesus said] "But so that we may not offend them, go to the lake and throw out your line. Take the first fish you catch; open its mouth and you will find a four-drachma coin. Take it and give it to them for my tax and yours."
>
> Matthew 17:27

Sometimes we get to have good times, and sometimes not so good. Our emotions and moods go up and down according to our circumstances. But thank goodness, our Lord isn't moody.

Jesus Christ is the same yesterday and today and forever.

Hebrews 13:8

Thumper

Everything's back to normal after our trip—
Joe went out to the garage to finish varnishing our
cupboard doors, and I'm trying to get caught up on the
household chores. No matter what else goes on, one thing
is certain: I have to cook—and then comes the cleanup.
Thank goodness for a dishwasher. I spent most of my life
without one and now I wouldn't exchange it for any
other appliance—except maybe the garbage disposal.

I have a few things against the dishwasher, though.
You still have to put all the food away, scrape the plates,
rinse off the silver, and scour the pans. At least I have to
with my dishwasher. They claim the newest ones do it
all with no effort on one's part, but mine is not about to
clean off sticky gravy or runny eggs, without help from
me.

I think it has a mean streak, too. I've never quite
learned how it likes to be loaded, but I do my best. First, I
place the plates between the little rubber-covered slots.
Then smaller plates and saucers. Bowls fit in the rounded
grooves; cups and glasses line up nicely in the top tray.
Plenty of holders for silverware. Pots and pans toward

the back on the bottom shelf. Close it, start it, and voilà! From somewhere inside it growls, *thumpity-thump, thumpity-thump*. What is going on? A lid assaulting a pan? Two plates having an argument?

So I yank it open, adjust the plates and bowls, push on the pans, jiggle the silverware. Try it again.

Thumpity-thump, thumpity-thump.

With my glasses so steamed up I can't see, I move the big bowls to the back and put the pans in front. Plates and bowls change places. Close it.

And now it wails, *thumpity-thump-BAM, thumpity-thump-BAM!*

While it's running, I usually go outside and water the plants because I've learned from experience that I might as well let the thing thump and bang its way to the clanking end. It's never going to let me find out what's thumping, anyhow.

I'm sure there's a lesson here for me—something about accepting life as it comes, or trying harder, or being patient. All I know right now is that Thumper is a mixed blessing.

"But he knows the way that I take; when he has tested me, I will come forth as gold."

Job 23:10

Maybe by the time Thumper wears out, the new dishwashers will not only scrub pans but will have a device that holds things so tight they can't thump.

No discipline seems pleasant at the time, but painful. Later on, however, it produces a harvest of righteousness and peace for those who have been trained by it.

Hebrews 12:11

Phony Phone Calls

Dinner was over, the dishes done, and I'd just settled down with Joe to watch "A Current Affair" when the telephone rang. Joe didn't make a move, so I struggled to my feet and hustled to answer it.

"Hi, there!" (A familiar voice.) "Is Joe there?" Somebody from church, probably.

"Just a minute."

Sighing, Joe lumbered to the phone. "Hello. Who? Not interested!" Bang went the receiver. He scowled at me. "Why did you call me to the phone? It was just some jerk, selling insurance." He plopped in his chair. "Why don't you tell those people we're not interested?"

"How did I know? He called you 'Joe.' I thought it was one of the trustees."

I had no sooner sat down than the phone rang again. "Hello?"

"Is this Mab?"

"Yes ... "

"This is Carol."

Carol? Carol who? I frantically tried to remember who Carol was.

"I'm with the 'Save the Pink Rose in Nantucket League,' and I was wondering if you'd help us out this month with a donation?"

"No, I give about all ..."

"Please don't say no until you hear me out." During the next five minutes she gave me her sales pitch.

I kept glancing in at the television, knowing that something exciting was being told on "A Current Affair."

"I'm sorry, but I can't ..."

"Hang up!" Joe exhorted.

I finally did ease the phone into its cradle while she was still talking.

Joe shook his head. "Honey, just tell these people we're not interested and hang up."

"I can't do that! What if the caller is someone we might meet at church? Or some neighbor, and they'd remember our name, and know I was the one who was hateful? They're people like us, trying to make a living."

His jaw jutted out. "Not on my phone during prime time."

Do not forget to entertain strangers, for by so doing some people have entertained angels without knowing it.

Hebrews 13:2

Tonight, when the phone rang at the start of "Father Dowling," I glanced at Joe, then snatched up the phone, and said, "Not interested!" I couldn't enjoy the show, wondering who it was.

Therefore, as God's chosen people ... clothe yourselves with compassion, kindness, humility, gentleness and patience.

Colossians 3:12

Dissatisfied

This hasn't been the best morning. First, Joe brought in a finished cabinet door to install. He was grinning with pride, but I was so disappointed I couldn't conceal it.

"It's too dark!" I moaned. "And it doesn't match the one you did before we went to Lodi!"

His lips were tight as he moved over to the window for a better look. In the process he accidentally kicked Samson's food dish, and kibbles flew like buckshot around the kitchen floor. He glared at me. "What's the cat's dish doing in the middle of the floor?"

"Because I *fed* him there!" I grabbed a broom and began to sweep up the pellets.

"I suppose if he'd wanted to have his snack in our bed, you'd put the dish there."

Before I could retort, I stumbled over Josephine's dish and sprayed more kibbles around the room.

After I cleaned up the mess and put away the broom, he said, "You didn't even notice how smoothly the varnish went on." I went over to the window and looked at the newly finished door. It was as smooth as if it were a professional job. He looked at me, his blue eyes worried. "Do you really think it's darker than the other one?"

"Well—" I remembered all the hard work he'd already done, sanding each door and drawer to take off the dark, almost-black varnish. And then, with what care he had put on this new finish. Maybe it wasn't *that* dark. It was just that I had my heart set on honey-colored cabinets. "Can you make the first one darker?"

"I don't know. Stain and varnish are tricky."

"It's okay, Honey." I gave him the best smile I could muster, considering how dissatisfied I was. "You really did a great job on the varnishing."

By the next evening he had all the doors and drawers finished and installed. Just as he twisted the last screw in place, Larita came in.

"Wow! Is it ever lighter and brighter in here!" She touched a door lightly. "They're beautiful!" Turning to me she said, "Boy, are you lucky to have Joe! I've wanted my cupboards done for ages." She bopped Joe on the arm. "Hey, you want to come do mine?"

Come to think of it, the cupboards *are* beautiful— and I'd better let Joe know that I think so.

... I have learned to be content whatever the circumstances.

Philippians 4:11

I still don't know why Joe didn't understand what I meant when I said "honey-colored." He must have gotten it mixed up with molasses.

Do not grumble.

1 Corinthians 10:10

Be content with what you have, because God has said, "Never will I leave you; never will I forsake you."

Hebrews 13:5

Women's Retreat

My dear friend, Rhea, just sent me a note inviting me to go on a women's retreat. I guess I'm getting old, but the thought of two nights in a dorm with ten screaming, giggling, game-playing women doesn't thrill me. A few years ago I would have jumped at the chance to spend a weekend in the mountains with her, but I still remember the pain of getting up at five-thirty after a nearly sleepless night, to take a two-mile nature hike to reach a wet meadow for morning devotions. When I was younger, I could tromp around all day at work in high heels, then shop all evening at the mall. For years I did aerobics for thirty minutes a day, but now I want to be comfortable, which preference causes me to stay in Reeboks and sweats a good part of the day.

On a retreat you don't have any control over the weather, either. I just hate to be too hot. Or too cold. Give me air conditioning in the summer and my electric blanket in the winter. And no bugs.

Still, it would be great to be with Rhea. We hardly ever get to visit anymore because we live so far apart. But I can't get the remembrance out of my mind of the last retreat I attended: The bunks had lumpy pads that weren't quite thick enough to disguise the flat springs. The furnace came on every fifteen minutes, and in my sleeping bag I was so hot I had to put my legs outside. I'm positive that a mouse (or worse) ran over my foot. The woman in the bunk above me snored *all* night, and the young lady on my right cried and blew her nose a lot. Ten of us shared the bath, and in the morning five lined up for the toilet, and the other five waited to use the one electrical outlet. The well-known speaker I was so looking forward to hearing got sick and didn't show.

Still, Rhea and I aren't getting any younger, and this is a great opportunity to be together. I guess I'll go. Hope the speaker isn't boring, and that the bed is soft. Just let me check the calendar. What's this? That's the weekend Cathy wants me to take care of the girls. Wow! What a (mixed) blessing!

He did what was right in the eyes of the Lord,
but not wholeheartedly.

2 Chronicles 25:2

Maybe I'm too concerned about my own comfort. And yet, we're supposed to take care of our bodies. Wonder which would be easier for me — go on the retreat or have the grandkids?

[Paul said], "I beat my body and make it my slave."

1 Corinthians 9:27

67

Linen Closet

Every wash day I have to push and struggle to make room in the linen closet for the clean towels because it is already stuffed full. Every shelf is piled with sheets, pillowslips, tablecloths, blankets, pillows, towels—plus several old picture frames. I used to keep the frames under the guest bed, but when Bob, Bonnie, and Kevin came down I figured I'd better move them. I put the frames in between the blankets in the linen closet until I could decide whether to keep them or give them to the missionaries. I still can't make up my mind whether to get rid of them or not. Frames are expensive, and some still have relatives' pictures in them—and you never know when they might come for a visit and expect to see themselves on display.

I'm glad I made up my mind to clean out the linen closet today. Then I might have room in it to put some of the Christmas decorations that I've kept under our bed ever since Joe claimed he didn't have room in the garage for them. As big as that garage is, you'd think there'd be room for some of my important things, yet, he fusses at me for storing things under our bed.

"You've got all kinds of cupboard space for stuff like that," he always says. "It just doesn't seem right to me to put things under the bed. My mother never did."

Frankly, I don't see anything wrong with it. The duster and bedspread hide everything. And if I don't keep it there, I'll just have to vacuum under the bed all the time. Work, work, work.

Well, I might as well get started on the linen closet. I think the first thing I'll do is hide the picture frames somewhere in the garage. Then I can move the decorations that are now under the bed to the linen closet, and that will please Joe. After all, as a Christian, I should try to be an obedient wife.

"Wives, submit to your husbands, as to the Lord. For the husband is the head of the wife as Christ is the head of the church, his body, of which he is the Savior.

Ephesians 5:22–23

I just had a good idea! Wonder if Joe would notice if I put the decorations behind the couch?

For God is not a God of disorder but of peace.

1 Corinthians 14:33

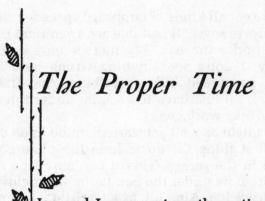

The Proper Time

Joe and I were out on the patio, enjoying a warm spring morning. I wanted to stay outside and work in the flower beds but had a ton of housework to do. I sighed wistfully. "If you could have anything you want, and money were no problem—what would you get?"

"Somebody to trim the olive tree—why?"

"I think I'd hire a housekeeper. Somebody to do everything inside so I could stay out here."

He chuckled. "It would never work, Babe."

"What do you mean?"

"Remember last year when you were sick that week and we hired a woman to clean the house? You got out of bed with a fever and mopped the kitchen floor before she came."

"Yeah. Well, I couldn't let anybody see how sticky the floor was."

"And remember," Joe went on, "when Maureen was going to help you clean house so you could work on the church newsletter? You spent most of the day cleaning ahead of her."

"But it's embarrassing for somebody at church to know—"

"—that we're human?" He took a swig of coffee. "Everybody gets toothpaste and hair in the washbasin."

I shuddered. "I still think it would be nice to have a housekeeper. You and I are the messiest people in the world."

He grinned and patted my hand. "Might as well relax and enjoy it."

I stood up and looked at the mountains. Cucamonga Peak against a blue sky was a picture postcard. "What a beautiful day! Makes you feel close to the Lord." I went over to the rose bed and discovered tiny green leaves sprouting out all over the pruned limbs. Bless their hearts! They should be fertilized. In front of them a few glads had poked slender blades out of the earth. And it was time to plant sweet peas and zinnias! I couldn't wait to feel the warm earth.

I thought of the laundry, the dishes on the counter, and the front room, messy with papers and last night's snack plates. Sadly, I turned toward the back door.

"Where you going?" Joe called.

Suddenly I thought of Mary and Martha. Was I Martha? Phooey on housework!

Grinning, I answered, "To get my gardening gloves."

"Martha, Martha," the Lord answered, "you are worried and upset about many things, but only one thing is needed. Mary has chosen what is better."

Luke 10:41—42

Still—should I put one load of clothes in before I start gardening? Stack the dishwasher? Run the vacuum?

The wise heart will know the proper time. . . .
For there is a proper time and procedure for
every matter.

Ecclesiastes 8:5—6

Lids

This morning I reached in the cupboard and picked up a container of raisins. As I started toward the counter, the lid came off in my hand, and the plastic jar dropped, spilling raisins all over the floor. With cats in the house, you know what that means, so I had to sweep up the raisins and throw them away.

"Bet I know how you did that," Joe taunted.

"It was an accident." I stared at him, wide-eyed.

"But it could have been avoided if a certain woman I know had screwed the lid on tighter."

"Well! A certain man *I* know screws everything down so tight I can never get it off! Anyway, it wasn't a screw-on lid. It was a snap-on, and it's not my fault if they don't always work right."

But he was right. No matter if lids are screw-on or snap-on, I seldom put them on right. I don't know why. I could claim it's because I have arthritis now and things are hard to open, but the truth is, I've been a lax-lid person all my life. I think it must stem from childhood difficulties with lids. When Mother made jelly, she always poured about an inch of paraffin wax on top to seal it. Unlike my Aunt Mab, who put her jelly in pretty jelly glasses, Mother always had to use an assortment of odd-shaped jars. The paraffin spread out below the neck, making it almost impossible to remove it without spurting jelly up in the air. She did a lot of home-canning, too, and used quart jars with big metal screw-on tops and rubber rings. The only way you could open them was to beat all around the edge of the lid with a knife handle. I think, since it was so hard to open containers as a child, I've learned to make it easy on myself. For example, I use raisins in oatmeal almost every morning, so why bother to put the lid on tight and cause myself extra work? I wouldn't want to admit this to Joe, but this slovenly practice has caused me quite a bit of extra work. Sweeping the floor this morning before breakfast was bad enough, but raisins are sticky little pixies, so I also had to mop. Last Sunday morning the lid came off the coffee can, resulting in coffee grounds all over the counter. That same morning, the orange juice container with a loose lid somehow got overturned in the fridge. Mess! Though it is nice to have the counter and fridge clean, Sunday morning isn't the best time for deep cleaning.

I wonder if this lid thing is bothering Joe? I think I'll talk to him. If he'll agree not to screw things down so tightly, I'll agree to put them on a little more tightly.

Wisdom is better than folly, just as light is better than darkness.

Ecclesiastes 2:13

I should just keep the coffee and the raisins on the counter, then I wouldn't have to worry about the lids.

Whoever heeds correction shows prudence.

Proverbs 15:5

Life of the Party

It was a sunny Saturday morning and I had gone out the front door to see if any of the plants I'd set out around our big tree were in bloom. Across the street some of our neighbors were standing around, talking. I waved at them, and pretty soon they wandered over to our lawn. Joe came outside, too, drinking coffee. All of us were joking and laughing about our bouts with flowers and fertilizers, bugs and blights. Most of the neighbors are witty and joke around a lot, and for some reason that morning I thought of many funny things to say. Almost every remark made them all laugh. I knew at the time some of the things I blurted out weren't exactly for Sunday school. In fact, I remember seeing a look of startled surprise on one of the women, but having your jokes laughed at is a heady experience, and I couldn't stop. Joe caught my eye a couple of times with a somber shake of his head, but my mind seemed to present even funnier, although questionable, one-liners.

When all went back to their yards, Joe said, "You really wowed them, didn't you?"

I didn't detect any praise in his voice. I felt guilty as I

remembered some of the off-color remarks I'd made. "I guess I got carried away."

"I was thinking about carrying you away, if you had gotten much worse."

"Did I say anything really—bad?"

Joe shrugged. "Not *bad* bad, but some of your jokes shouldn't have come from a Christian."

I felt miserable. "I've told all of them about my faith in the Lord and how to be saved. Now I've probably ruined my testimony."

> Do not let any unwholesome talk come out of your mouths, but only what is helpful for building others up according to their needs, that it may benefit those who listen.
>
> Ephesians 4:29

O Lord, please forgive me! But why is it that some of the funniest things that come to mind are not wholesome?

> And do not grieve the Holy Spirit of God, with whom you were sealed for the day of redemption.
>
> Ephesians 4:30

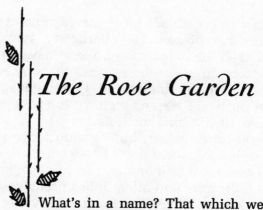

The Rose Garden

What's in a name? That which we call a rose
by any other name would smell as sweet.
—William Shakespeare

Because roses are my favorite flower, wherever we
have lived I have had a rose garden. They aren't the
easiest flowers to grow. They require a great deal of work,
beginning with digging holes big enough for the roots to
spread out. I've always taken care of my roses until we
moved here. I couldn't wait to buy rosebushes and set
them out, but when I put the shovel in the ground and
tried to push on it with my foot, I almost fell over. It was
like digging in concrete, because of rocks underneath the
topsoil. A neighbor who was watching me struggle came
over.

"Doubt you'll be able to dig in that ground."

"I'm finding that out. Everywhere I try to dig there's
a rock."

"This tract was built on a riverbed. That's why."

When Joe came back from visiting his mom that
afternoon, I told him it was impossible for us to have
roses here.

"Nothing's impossible," he declared, and went to the garage for his pickax. He alternately swung the pickax and soaked the holes, mumbling something about pouring concrete in the whole area. By sunset, and dripping with sweat, he finally dug up enough rocks to set out seven bushes. I wanted eight in the rose garden, but he refused to dig another hole.

Roses need much water, but as soon as you water them, grass begins to grow. I don't know where the seeds come from. There must be a hundred forty-seven kinds of grass here in California and all varieties prefer rose beds to any other ground. Some I've fought are water grass, bunch grass, bamboo and foxtail grass, but the most tenacious one is crabgrass. I'm sure it's called that because it makes people so crabby. It starts with one tiny blade, usually hidden at the very base of a rosebush so that you tear your arm on thorns if you try to pull it out, and two days later a long runner snakes out, quickly finding root even in this rocky soil—then it sends another runner . . . and another. Two weeks of neglect and the garden can be covered with the wiry stuff. For some reason, none of these grasses do well in our lawn. We have to struggle as hard to get grass to grow as we do to keep it out of the rose beds.

Probably the worst thing of all about growing roses is aphids. These ugly, little green critters somehow endure winter, and as soon as the rosebushes begin to sprout new growth, they take over. They stick their noses into the tender leaves and suck juice all day. They secrete a sticky, syrupy stuff that attracts ants and bees, which sting humans. I learned several years ago, after being stung, to look carefully inside a rose before sniffing it.

After fighting grass and aphids, it is thrilling to see

rosebuds beginning to form. But then another problem arises: thrip—a condition caused by even tinier juice-sucking insects that attack rosebuds so that when the blossom opens it looks like somebody took a bite out of it.

Rosebushes, to keep blooming, have to be pruned every January, to which surgery the bushes not only resist but fight back. The thorn-covered branches are stubborn and tough, and although I wear gloves, by the time I've pruned all seven, my arms and sometimes my face look as though I've been in a cat fight.

I try not to let Joe know about all these little problems because his opinion of the rose garden is low anyway. "I can't understand why you're so crazy about roses," he says over and over. "You can't get near the dumb things without being stuck."

But oh, the beauty of roses—my favorite flower—is worth all the pain and work.

I am a rose of Sharon, a lily of the valleys.
Song of Songs 2:1

Why couldn't my favorite flower be dandelions?

The grass withers and the flowers fall, but the word of our God stands forever.
Isaiah 40:8

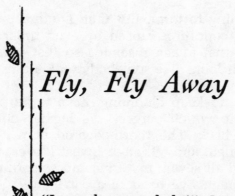

Fly, Fly Away

 "I need some help!" I called. Ron and Barbara with their three kids, and Don and Joan with their three, had come over after church to share Mother's Day with us. "If you all carry out something, maybe we can eat before the flies discover us. Hurry!"

On the patio Ron placed a dish of potato salad on the table. "Are the flies that bad, Mother?"

"They're terrible this year. I think they're demon-possessed." Our preacher son laughed indulgently. "No, I'm serious," I insisted. "They sneak in the house without even a door's being opened. But just let me pick up a flyswatter and they're gone!"

"I don't blame them!" Joan winked at her brother. "When Mother has the flyswatter, she's dangerous!"

"Oh, no," Don groaned. "Flies buzzing around are better than all the food knocked over."

Barbara touched my arm. "Mom, remember the time you knocked over that vase of flowers—"

"Let's ask the blessing," Joe cut in. "Maybe they won't find us for a while."

After Ron asked the blessing, Judi said, "Grandmother, tell us about the time Aunt Mab killed a fly with a knife."

"Well, we were camping at Big Bear," I began, "and were all sitting at a big wooden picnic table, having breakfast. Aunt Mab picked up her knife and held it like a cleaver as she watched a fly buzzing around her pancakes. 'What are you going to do with the knife, Aunt Mab?' Aunt Sissy asked.

"Without taking her blue eyes off it she said, 'I'm going to kill this fly.' Suddenly, like a lizard whipping out his tongue, she whacked off that fly's head! In midair!"

"And while we were all staring at the decapitated fly," Joan added, "she calmly went back to eating, as though she cut off flies' heads every day."

"Wow," Danny said. "What's the success rate of killing a fly like that?"

"I have no idea," I answered. "She told me later that she was as surprised as we were when she actually hit it."

We were almost through our meal when the flies found us. Big green things, flying slowly over our food, touching down for a second or two as they decided which delicacy they wanted to eat. As they sprinted around the table, stopping sometimes to groom themselves with their hind legs, or insolently sniff someone's plate, I could feel my temperature rise. They were ruining my Mothers Day! When I grabbed the flyswatter, Don covered his eyes and moaned, "Mab, be calm. Please!"

A big and arrogant one landed on the edge of the fruit salad bowl. Before anyone could stop me, I smacked it, and it toppled over on top of a piece of pineapple.

Everybody groaned. David muttered, "Gross, Grandmother!" Laurie left the table. Barbara looked stricken. Timmy grinned and raised his thumb. "Way to go!"

"Grandmother," Jeni scolded, "flies flying around aren't as bad as squished ones!"

We had our dessert indoors, but I think everyone had a loss of appetite. Maybe I shouldn't have killed that fly, but flies make me lose my senses. Oh, why did God make flies?

> Through him all things were made; without him nothing was made that has been made.
>
> John 1:3

I know the Lord has a purpose for flies — fortunately, one of them won't be fulfilling its purpose.

> As dead flies give perfume a bad smell, so a little folly outweighs wisdom and honor.
>
> Ecclesiastes 10:1

Old Glory

On Memorial Day, Joe and I went out on the porch together to hang the American flag. After the pole was in its slot and the flag waving, Joe and I saluted it. Sometimes we even say the Pledge of Allegiance. Joe grinned self-consciously. "Our neighbors probably think we're nuts when we salute the flag." He looked up and down the quiet street. "Not many people put out a flag anymore."

"Flags were flying every day during 'Desert Storm'—the stores ran out of them!"

"I'm sure you can buy a flag now."

"I'm sure. But some of our neighbors are young. With prices so high, it's probably all they can do to pay the rent and put food on the table . . ."

"Much less buy a flag," he finished.

"You know that wedding we're going to in June? How about buying them a flag?"

"For a wedding present?"

"Why not? They'll probably get two or three toasters, and clocks, and towels—I'll bet nobody buys them an American flag!"

"I'll bet you're right." He gave me a knowing look. "Put yourself in their place. When we first got married, would you have been glad to get a flag?"

"I seriously doubt it."

"I think it's a good idea! We can buy the kind with a pole and the eagle thing on top."

He shook his head. "How will you wrap it? Or will you just march into the church with the banner unfurled? Maybe the organist could play the 'Star Spangled Banner.'"

"Come on! We're supposed to take the gift to the bride's house before the wedding."

"Okay. I'll let you make that delivery by yourself."

"I can't believe you. You're a veteran! Don't you love our country?"

"Of course. I'm just not sure a flag is a good wedding present."

I looked up at our flag gently rippling in the morning breeze. It represented America—our wonderful, free, Christian nation. But maybe it wasn't a good wedding gift. I tried to visualize the couple as they opened presents—tablecloths, dishes, towels, crystal—a *flag*? I sighed as I turned to go back in the house.

"Where you going?" Joe asked.

"To look at the ads and see what's on sale in the way of wedding presents."

But you are a chosen people . . . a holy nation, a people belonging to God, that you may declare the praises of him who called you out of darkness into his wonderful light.

1 Peter 2:9

84

I still think the American flag is a good wedding gift. Maybe I could buy a small one to decorate the gift.

We will shout for joy ... and will lift up our banners in the name of our God.

Psalm 20:5

Too Soon

We were watching the evening news and I could feel Joe glance at me, then at the TV, then back at me. "Well?" I asked.

"I was just wondering why you're wrapped up in that beach towel?"

"Because I'm freezing to death," I snapped.

"Why don't you put on a sweater?"

I frowned. He *would* have to ask. "Because they're all put away, and I'm not about to tear open the plastic bags. They're all neat and Scotch-taped and—"

"Okay, okay." He tried to look serious. "You did it again, huh?"

I grunted. I *had* done it again. "But don't you remember how hot it was in March when I put the winter clothes away?" I tucked the towel around my legs. "It was *ninety* for a few days."

"I remember. The cats started shedding . . . ants got in the sugar."

"We even had to use the air conditioner! Every spring we have a hot spell and I'm tricked into putting away the winter clothes and dragging out the summer stuff." I tucked a sofa pillow on my feet. "It's not easy, either, putting away the winter clothes in garment bags and the sweaters and jackets in plastic bags, sealing them up against moths, and lugging them to the front closet."

Joe nodded sympathetically, but he still had a maddening twinkle in his eyes. "Want me to turn on the furnace?"

"No. It would stink." I shivered. "But it always happens. Here it is June and it's freezing! Who knows how long it will last. I'll probably be forced to open up the plastic bags, drag out sweaters, jackets, and sweat suits—"

"In September it's the same thing in reverse," Joe said. "We have an early storm, have to start using the furnace—"

"Quit grinning at me! I know I put away all the shorts and cool things too soon last fall. When we had that heat wave in October, I was running around in my slip. I'll never learn."

He looked sad. "Honey, why don't you get in bed and turn up the electric blanket?"

I bit my lip. "I can't! I put it away, too."

He who scorns instruction will pay for it.

Proverbs 13:13

I know from experience that I might as well get out the warm clothes and the electric blanket, too. There might even be snow in the morning.

Wait for the Lord; be strong and take heart and wait for the Lord.

Psalm 27:14

Tale of Three Sisters

Joe looked at his watch, then out the window. "Cathy and Bill and the kids should be here pretty soon."

I opened the oven and took out a sizzling roast. "Hope so. Everything's ready."

When Cathy and Bill come, we let them have our bedroom and Joe and I sleep in the motor home. Chrystal, eight, and Nicole, six, share the front bedroom; Melissa, three, sleeps in the back bedroom. We hide all the no-no foods, and put perfumes and treasures up high. We were all ready now and looking forward to this visit.

Outside, a door slammed; then another and another. A tiny tap-tap sounded and we opened the door. There they were! Chrystal, blue-eyed, long blond hair, tight jeans and boots—Nicole, brown eyes and long brown hair, checked pants and lace-trimmed sweatshirt. And Melissa! Hazel-eyed, blond wispy hair, pink sweats, one pantleg up to her knee. That beautiful picture framed in the doorway suddenly turned into a fast-forward movie.

Chrystal: "Grandmother, where are the cats?"

Nicole: "Grandmudda, I'm thirsty."

Melissa: "Go potty now!"

Chrystal: "Grandmother, did you know our soccer team is the best?"

Nicole: "I want juice and a banana."

Melissa: *"Potty!"*

Chrystal: "Can we play Parcheesi now? Will you teach me to knit?"

Nicole: "I know! Let's have pizza?"

Melissa was suddenly quiet as she waddled across the living room.

Bill bustled in with luggage under both arms. Cathy pushed in with a mini ice chest and sacks of food. "Chrystal!" Her voice carried above the constant chatter. "Help Daddy put the stuff in the right rooms. Nicole, stop asking for food! Melissa—*Melissa!* How could you?"

After dinner I had just sprawled on the couch by Cathy, ready for some adult conversation, when Nicole brought me the curlers and comb. The girls love to play beauty shop, with me as the only patron. So much for adult conversation. Cathy was asleep, and the men were watching the eight o'clock movie.

Sitting on the floor, I relaxed while Chrystal powdered my face until we were all sneezing. Next came blusher, then lipstick. Nicole attacked my hair as though it were an unpleasant chore that had to be done, rolling and twisting the curlers into a tangled mess. Melissa, who thinks she can do anything her older sisters can, did her share of pulling and wrapping my hair. Her special expertise was applying eyeshadow before I could close my eyes.

When the movie was about half over, Cathy roused, took one looked at me and howled, then grabbed her camera.

After snapping my picture, she hustled the girls into their rooms, for pajamas. About ten o'clock after a few arguments, snacks, and drinks, the house was quiet.

At last Cathy and I could talk—but I was too tired.

In the motor home Joe said, "Think you can take another day and night?"

"Are you kidding? I *adore* them." Groaning softly, I fell into bed. "But don't you dare let them in here in the morning until I say so."

Sons (daughters) are a heritage from the Lord,
children a reward from him.

Psalm 127:3

When the girls were "setting" my hair, the thought crossed my mind that the retreat might have been more relaxing.

Jesus said, "Let the little children come to me, and do not hinder them, for the kingdom of heaven belongs to such as these."

Matthew 19:14

90

Chloë

Chloë is one of my neighbors, and I'm sure that the Lord has appointed her to develop Christian graces in me. The first time I met her was the day we moved in. Joe and I were taking a coffee break out on our "new" patio, admiring our swimming pool and thanking the Lord for letting us find a home at a price we could afford. Suddenly, a curler-crested head popped up on the six-foot-high block wall.

"Hi!" she said, resting her chin on chubby bare arms. "Whatcha guys doin'?" Her voice was a cross between a dog's bark and a parrot's squawk. I was so startled that I couldn't answer. *She must have a ladder on the other side,* I thought.

"Can I go swimmin' this summer? The other people used to let me swim anytime I wanted."

Joe spoke quietly to me, scarcely moving his lips. "Not playing with a full deck."

"What's your name?" she croaked but didn't wait for an answer. "My name's Chloë and my son's name is Arnold. He's retarded. He's sick with the flu, and I don't have the money to take him to a doctor, and the old man won't give me any." For the next five minutes she rattled on, jumping from subject to subject, never giving us a chance to reply. Since I couldn't get a word in, I picked up my coffee cup, waved at her, went in the house, and Joe followed me.

Indoors, a great lump of anger welled up inside me and I burst into tears. "No wonder this darling house, *with a pool*, was so cheap," I moaned. "The former owners were desperate to get away from that—that goofball!"

In the next year she "borrowed" but never paid back—sugar, laundry detergent, cooking oil, milk, vanilla, potatoes, and carrots. Every time she came over she had a long, disjointed story to tell.

One day after she left with a full pitcher of syrup, Joe exploded. "You're going to have to set her straight, Babe."

"But if I make her mad, I can never tell her about the Lord."

"The way she talks you'll never get a chance anyway."

One day she borrowed two carrots for soup she was making. Scrounging up all my courage, I said, "Okay, Chloë, but you've got to pay me back. I need them."

Her brown eyes widened in surprise. Evidently the concept of paying me back had never occurred to her. However, that evening she brought two carrots to me. I invited her in and decided to try to tell her about the Lord. "Chloë, do you believe in Jesus?"

"My old man don't. He won't talk about it, or give me any money, or—"

"Chloë, listen a minute. The Lord loves you. Okay?

92

Jesus died to save you. Do you believe that? He'll forgive your sins."

She stared at me. It was the first time she didn't have anything to say.

After a moment she went to the door. "I'm gonna start paintin' the bedroom maybe tomorrow—"

I eased her out the door. She talked to herself all the way home.

"Lord Jesus," I whispered, "I tried."

For I resolved to know nothing while I was with you except Jesus Christ and him crucified.

1 Corinthians 2:2

I feel so guilty! I know I'm supposed to love my neighbor. I guess I ought to invite her to go swimming.

I planted the seed, Apollos watered it, but God made it grow. So neither he who plants nor he who waters is anything, but only God, who makes things grow.

1 Corinthians 3:6—7

Cross My Fingers

Over the past few weeks I've burned a pot of beans, left the water running on the lawn, driven away and left the garage door open, and missed my best friend's birthday! Joe says it's because I don't concentrate, but while I'm trying to concentrate, my mind starts thinking of other things. I have learned to set the timer when I cook, but I guess I wasn't concentrating the day I burned the beans. Circling calendar dates works for some people. At the first of the year I always circle birthdays and dates on the calendar, but that doesn't make me look at it. I also faithfully make lists but forget to look at them.

Fortunately, I realized that this concentration problem of mine wasn't getting better and that I would have to take steps to thwart myself. I'm happy to report that for the past two weeks I haven't burned anything, forgotten a birthday, or forgotten to take my list to the store. The secret of my success is *memory joggers.*

My favorite is *crossed fingers.* This is for times when I want to heat something on the burner for just a minute or two and I don't want to bother with the timer. I just cross my middle finger over the index finger on my left

94

hand and leave it until the time is up. This works equally well when you want to leave the water running outside for a couple of minutes, or if you want to take something out of the dryer before the other clothes are dry. Keeping your fingers crossed isn't especially comfortable; in fact, it's a nuisance if you are eating or combing your hair, but it does work.

Object-in-front-of-the-door is another good memory jogger. Suppose that you want to return a library book, or not forget your lunch—just put it in front of the door. The only way this won't work is if you go out the other door, or some neat family member picks it up and puts it away.

When crossed fingers are not practical, I've had success employing a *note and toothbrush*. I used to have trouble remembering to put out the trash Friday mornings until I wrote a note, PUT OUT TRASH, and taped it to my toothbrush. I use this method often, and the only time it didn't work was when I wrote, "Don't forget"— but couldn't remember what I was supposed to remember.

Other tactics I've used: putting a glass tumbler upside down in the center of the counter before going to bed. That alerts me to get hamburger out of the freezer. When I want to remember to make a doctor's appointment, I put a loaf of bread by the phone. When I find the bread, I remember to call the doctor.

One thing I can't seem to concentrate on is my glasses. When we're ready to leave the house, Joe almost always asks, "Do you have your glasses?" But if he forgets, then I leave them at home. I don't think he's impressed yet with my concentration. He told me yesterday to buy a chain so that I could wear my glasses around my neck.

> You are to make tassles on the corners of your garments ... so you will remember all the commands of the Lord.
>
> Numbers 15:38—39

Maybe I just forget the things I don't want to remember. I certainly don't have any problem remembering my birthday, or Mother's Day, Valentine's Day, or our anniversary.

Only be careful, and watch yourselves closely so that you do not forget the things your eyes have seen or let them slip from your heart as long as you live. Teach them to your children and to their children after them.

Deuteronomy 4:9

Freezer

When I came back from the store and tried to put away the frozen food, I knew I was going to have to do something about the freezer. Our refrigerator was born in 1970, and although it has run almost perfectly (except for a time when a stack of newspapers fell into the cover at the back), the freezer compartment has always been too small. To put away the new orange juice, meat, and vegetables, I had to take out an open three-pound can of coffee and two loaves of bread. Even then, I had to keep pounding things back in with a rolling pin. Frozen packages kept sliding out, bonking me on the face and arms, and a big plastic-wrapped thing came tumbling out and landed on my foot. It was all of our important papers I had put in there for safekeeping in case of fire.

One reason I had such a bad time is that ever since Joe moved the refrigerator out on the back porch, I haven't been able to open either the freezer or refrigerator doors all the way because the space between the front of the fridge and the wall isn't quite big enough. It's no real problem on a daily basis, except that I tend to sort of toss things in instead of placing them in an orderly manner.

To be truthful, they never were that orderly, but at least I could prop the doors wide open and see what I had.

I know that the first time I try to open the freezer it will be like an avalanche again, so I guess I'll work on it tomorrow morning and see if I can't make room to get the coffee and bread back in there.

It's all done! I took everything out and washed the compartment with ammonia water. I hadn't planned on all that, but it was a sticky mess. At some time or other, chocolate ice cream had melted and run all over the bottom and then frozen again. Stuck in it, in sort of a collage effect, were a few peas and some kernel corn. Toward the back, frozen in an upright position, was one fish stick. Anyway, it's all nice and clean now, and everything is back in—even our important papers, the coffee, and bread.

I will have to cook the chuck roast and hamburger today. There wasn't room for it even when I pounded it with the rolling pin.

But everything should be done in a fitting and orderly way.

1 Corinthians 14:40

Maybe I should take out the two-pound box of chocolates I have hidden in the back of the freezer and share them with Joe.

A wife of noble character is her husband's crown, but a disgraceful wife is like decay in his bones.

Proverbs 12:4

98

Neighbors

Joe and I were sitting on the front steps enjoying the evening breeze when it began. Chloë and Wilbur were having another fight. We couldn't help but hear what they were saying.

"Alls I'm good for is to cook," Chloë's raspy voice cranked out. "Why'n't you leave? You don't want me nohow."

"It's not my fault you didn't go to breakfast with us!" Wilbur shouted. "Remember, I asked you."

"I ain't going nowhere with your friends! You should be glad to take me."

"Where? To your mother's? You should go live with her!"

I leaned against Joe. "They're mad tonight!"

He nodded and put a finger to his lips.

"Why don't *you* go and live with your pals!" Chloë's voice was a screech. "I wisht you would!" There was a crash.

Joe stood up. "Let's go in! TV's not as violent."

Inside, I said, "You know what's wrong with them? They aren't compatible."

"You're kidding!"

"He shouldn't go running off with his friends so often."

Joe shrugged. "If you were like Chloë, I'd go out with the boys, too."

I smiled up at him. "Thank you for thinking I'm so sweet."

"I didn't mean that, exactly." He sat down on the couch and put his feet on the coffee table.

I frowned at him. "Well, what do you mean?"

"I mean that she's self-centered. Always talking about herself. She never gives anybody else a thought. And the way she hollers at him. Putting him down. A man doesn't like to be put down."

I sat beside him and squeezed his hand. "And I'm not like that, huh?" I kissed his cheek.

He looked down at me. "Not usually."

"What are you saying?"

He was silent for a moment. "Sometimes you're not as sweet and gentle as you used to be."

"Well! Maybe you aren't either!"

Do not repay evil with evil or insult with insult, but with blessing, because to this you were called so that you may inherit a blessing.

1 Peter 3:9

I can't believe he'd say that! It seems to me I'm always sweet!

But the fruit of the Spirit is love, joy, peace, patience, kindness, goodness, faithfulness, gentleness and self-control.

Galatians 5:22, 23

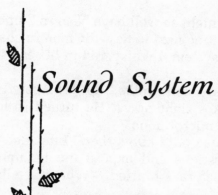

Sound System

Our church is building a new sanctuary and, because I directed the Christmas play one year, they asked me to serve on the lights and sound committee.

"I don't know anything about sound systems," I protested to Dennis, the chairman.

"You know about plays, and that involves sound, right?"

Our first meeting was at his house. Four of us gathered around a table, drinking strong coffee and studying blueprints. At least, *they* were studying. I couldn't tell the proposed narthex from the baptistry, but I tried to look intelligent, remembering my mother's advice: "If you don't talk, you won't expose your ignorance."

Dennis looked up from the blueprint and rolled a pencil back and forth between his palms. "Our job is to recommend a contractor to the board," he said, "so first, we have to determine what our needs are."

The men began a noisy discussion of what they thought we should have. They threw around such words as *condensers, amplifiers, vibrating coils, amps, patch bays,* and *PZMs.* I might as well have been in Zambia for all I understood. Sitting next to Ray, the man in charge of our present sound system, I whispered in his ear, "What are PZMs?"

"Means pressure zone mike," he whispered back. "We're talking mikes right now." He turned to look at me. "*Mike* means microphone."

I rolled my eyes up. "I know *that.*" I decided not to ask any more questions and expose my ignorance. A minute went by before I blurted, "What's a vibrating coil?"

Ray pursed his lips. "Well—" he began to explain. "The sound waves create pressure on a wafer—"

"A *wafer?*"

"Not a *wafer* wafer." He looked just a tad exasperated. "Something wafer thin." He shook his head slightly and turned back to the other men. He pointed at the blueprint. "Now the patch bay should be just about here." The others nodded. "So we're talking like fifty-two to fifty-five up on stage."

"And we'll have to have a mixer of at least thirty-two channels," Dennis added.

"But don't forget," Doug put in, "we need monitors. It's murder when the soloist can't hear."

I looked from one to the other. What was a patch bay? And fifty-two *what?* And thirty-two channels? Were we going to have TV hooked up to this stuff?

Ray said, "Any idea how many woofers and tweeters we should have?"

Woofers and *tweeters?* I couldn't keep quiet. "What are they?"

They all grinned as though I were a little old lady in

tennis shoes. Ray, tongue-in-cheek, explained, "A woofer is a great big doggie, and a tweeter is a little dog."

"You guys! I know you're making fun of me."

Dennis patted my hand. "We're talking about speakers, love. A woofer is a bass speaker, and a tweeter is for high frequency sounds."

Well, well, well! Even at my age I'm learning things.

Let the wise listen and add to their learning.
Proverbs 1:5

Won't Tim be amazed when I ask him how many woofers and tweeters are in his stereo!

A prudent man keeps his knowledge to himself, but the heart of fools blurts out folly.
Proverbs 12:23

Shoes on the Bed

We had just come in from our morning walk, hot and sweaty, and ready for showers. I sat down on the bed, took off my Reeboks, and placed them beside me on the bedspread.

Seated on a bench at the foot of the bed, Joe took off his shoes and tossed them toward the closet. He looked at my shoes then said, "I have a question for you."

Oh, oh. I looked at him suspiciously. "Yes?"

He pulled off his sweatshirt and tossed it in the general direction of the clothes hamper. "How come you always put your shoes on the bed when you take them off?"

I pushed them off the bed. "I don't *always*."

"Yes, you do. I've noticed. You come in, sit down on the bed, take off one shoe at a time, and put them on the bed." He reached for his bathrobe. "I don't care. You're the one that has to wash the bedspread. I just wonder why you do it."

I looked at my dusty clodhoppers, definitely out of place on top of our mint-green bedspread. Whoever heard of putting shoes on the bed? I would have spanked the kids for doing it. Why did I do it? And I wasn't even aware of doing it. I felt guilty, embarrassed, flustered, but this was no time to act guilty in front of him. I lifted my chin and looked him in the eye. "Well—I have my reasons."

"Like what?"

I made an impatient sound. "I don't know!" I pointed at his shoes. "Why do you leave your shoes where I stumble over them?" He shrugged and went into the bathroom. "At least they're on the floor where they belong."

While he was taking his shower, I put my shoes neatly in the closet. I also put his shoes away and tossed his sweatshirt, socks, and underwear in the hamper.

Shoes on the bed! When had I started doing that? I remembered last Sunday coming in from church, sitting down on the bed, and, exactly as he said, I took off my high heels and put them on the bed! Why?

Then I realized why. I'm getting old. It's easier on my aching back and legs to put the shoes on the bed. If I put them on the floor, then I have to lean over to pick them up, and that hurts! Mystery solved.

Why he leaves his shoes in the middle of the room is another mystery.

Then your arms, that have protected you, will tremble, and your legs, now strong, will grow weak.

Ecclesiastes 12:3 (TEV)

I must break myself of putting my shoes on the bed! Otherwise, how can I remind him that his shoes are in my way?

Even to your old age and gray hairs I am he, I am he who will sustain you.

Isaiah 46:4

105

Nintendo

"What can we do to amuse Kevin when he and Bonnie come down this weekend?" I said.

"Nobody amused me when I was six," Joe answered.

"Things are different now. All the grandkids have things to entertain them."

"I guess we can rent videos."

"I meant something of *value*—kids today have too much space-age stuff."

I needn't have worried about entertaining Kevin. When they arrived Friday night, Bonnie brought in a small TV.

"Why did you do that, Honey?" I said. "You know we have television."

"It's for his Nintendo game," she explained. "You guys will love it!"

Even though she had driven for eight hours and it was past Kevin's bedtime, she hooked up the game and Kevin flopped on his stomach, staring up at the colored screen where a little man named Mario was hopping across some bricks and pipes. A catchy computer tune accompanied the action, which Kevin regulated with a control pad. He kept working the buttons while his eyes never left the screen. After watching the cartoon-like character skitter around for a while, I tapped Kevin on the shoulder. "What's the object of the game?"

When he didn't answer, Bonnie explained. "Mario has to free Princess Toadstool from the bad guy, Koopa."

"Oh. Is that the Princess?"

"No! That's a Koopa Troopa."

"Want to play, Grandad?" Kevin grinned at Joe. "Of course, I'll beat you." His blue-green eyes twinkled. "I'm very good at this."

Joe, who is also very good at games, tried to put Mario through his paces, but the little fellow fell through a hole too many times, and the screen announced "Game Over."

"Want to try, Grandmother?"

Self-consciously I held the pad in my hand.

"The red button makes him jump," Kevin told me, "and the black thing makes it go left and right."

The first few steps were okay, then a rotten Little Goomba got Mario and the game was over for me, too.

Most of the next day Kevin played Nintendo, and I asked Bonnie if she thought he was playing too much. "Don't you think he should go outside a while?" After all, Joe and I wanted a turn. Finally, late in the afternoon, Kevin decided to watch "Back to the Future 3," so I grabbed the Nintendo control and tried again. And again. And again. Fascinating! But Mario and I never got over two blocks from home before we either fell in a hole, or were eaten by Koopa Troopas. I never did meet Lakitu, or Buzzy Beetle, or the great Koopa himself. Joe didn't do any better. I knew we needed more practice.

When we waved good-bye to Bonnie and Kevin

Monday morning, I said, "I know what I'm going to get you for your birthday, Joe. A Nintendo!"

When I was a child, I talked like a child, I thought like a child, I reasoned like a child. When I became a man, I put childish ways behind me.

1 Corinthians 13:11

With a little more practice, I'm sure I could rescue Princess Toadstool.

I tell you the truth, anyone who will not receive the kingdom of God like a little child will never enter it.

Mark 10:15

Miracle Floor

Before I even finished my cereal the day before yesterday, Joe moved the table and chairs out of the kitchen and started ripping up the old Congoleum rug. By noon he was ready to start laying the beautiful new white tiles. I insisted on helping, and we disagreed first thing.

"Why don't we start laying the tile along this wall?" I asked.

Using his father-to-child voice, he said, "The directions say we have to draw a plumb line lengthwise, then one across the width. Then we start in the center."

Working more or less harmoniously, we had the floor finished by eight that evening, and it looked great.

"My knees are killing me," I whimpered, limping to the hall closet to get the heating pad.

"It's not my knees as much as my back," Joe groaned as he hunched his shoulders. "Let's take aspirin and go to bed."

Sometime in the night I thought I heard water running, but I was too exhausted to get up. When the alarm went off, I rolled out, yawned, and headed for the kitchen to let the cats out. When I opened the door, I saw Samson and Josephine up on the table.

"Bad cats!" I clapped my hands. "Scat!" They huddled in the center of the table and refused to budge. Suddenly my bedroom slippers felt wet, and I realized I was standing in water. "Joe!" I shrieked as loud as I could. "Get up!"

Joe came yawning in, hair tousled, and barefoot. He squawked when ice cold water squished between his toes. Lifting his feet high, he tiptoed across the floor and looked under the sink where he discovered that one of the connections had come loose. Water had been pouring from it for hours.

After a half hour of frantic sweeping and mopping, we finally got most of the water out. We collapsed on kitchen chairs and looked around. "So much for all our work yesterday," Joe moaned. "Look at all those loose tiles." Some had even moved as much as an inch.

"Can't we stick them back down?" I began pushing tiles in place.

Joe shook his head. "After breakfast we might as well take them up and start over."

Tears rolled down my cheeks. "Dear Jesus, *why?*" It was more of a complaint than a prayer. "Why did this have to happen? All that hard work for nothing! Now we'll have to do it all over. Oh, Lord! Please help us!"

After a sad breakfast in the living room, we discovered that an amazing thing had happened! We couldn't budge any of the tiles! The water, if anything, had made them stick more tightly. "It's just temporary," Joe predicted. "Soon as the floor dries completely, they'll curl. We might as well pry them up and start gluing."

But this morning the floor still looks great, so I guess we'll wait another day. Maybe this is a miracle!

Now to him who is able to do immeasurably more than all we ask or imagine, according to his power that is at work within us, to him be glory in the church and in Christ Jesus throughout all generations, for ever and ever! Amen.
Ephesians 3:20–21

I'm not sure I'll tell anybody about praying for help. It seems too far out that God would care about our kitchen floor.

Then you will call upon me, and come and pray to me and I will listen to you.
Jeremiah 29:12

Empty

It was hot. I was hot. Joe had gone to attend to some business and I'd been working on the pool all morning trying to get it clean—as a surprise for him. Not only was I hot but I was hungry. *Wouldn't an Eskimo Pie taste good,* I thought. Smacking my lips, I rushed to the freezer and took out the Eskimo Pie carton. I couldn't wait to bite into a cold, smooth, chocolatey—Empty. EMPTY?! Gnashing my teeth, I tore the carton to shreds. "Joe!" I yelled into the air. "I'll never forgive you!" Why couldn't I teach that man elementary household procedures? It wasn't that I begrudged him an ice cream bar, but couldn't he tell me when he took the last one? Or, if he was too embarrassed to admit he'd been pig enough to eat the very last one without even offering me a bite, couldn't he have at least left the empty box on the counter where I'd be sure to see it? Why would he leave an empty box in the fridge?

The Eskimo Pie disappointment isn't his only empty-carton trick. I can't count the times I've been making a grocery list, looked in the cupboard at fat-looking boxes of cereal lined up, and decided I didn't need to buy any this time—only to discover at breakfast that the Shredded Wheat box contained a tablespoon of shreds, or that he'd eaten the very last Cheerio. Joe also has a skillful way of making the bread wrapper look half full when only a heel is left.

I never do that to him. I always say, "Honey, I'm eating the last piece of pie. Want some of it?" I try to be kind and considerate and generous. Although I have to admit that I'm a little devious when it comes to See's chocolates, I've learned how to take out all the empty paper cups and spread out what's left so that he doesn't know how many I've eaten. See's chocolates! I'd forgotten about them. I'd better go have a couple right now, or the next time I look I'll find an empty box.

Be kind and compassionate to one another, forgiving each other, just as in Christ God forgave you.

Ephesians 4:32

The next time I buy a carton of Eskimo Pies, I'm going to hide one just for myself way back behind the frozen hamburger.

All man's efforts are for his mouth, yet his appetite is never satisfied.

Ecclesiastes 6:7

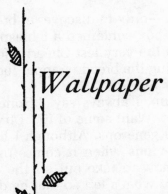

Wallpaper

"Ward's has all its wallpaper on sale for half price." I took the ad into the living room and handed it to Joe.

"What do you want to paper?"

"The kitchen. Everything else is new."

He shifted his toothpick. "Hanging paper isn't one of my gifts."

"I know. I will hang the paper."

At the store I chose a pre-pasted vinyl with a soft pearly background, lavender butterflies, and pale green leaves. "It's perfect to go with my African violets!"

At home I began to yank off the old paper. I couldn't wait to start. By bedtime, with Joe's help, the naked and patched wall was ready to be adorned.

The next morning I opened a roll of paper and tossed the directions in the wastebasket.

"If I were you, I'd read the directions," Joe warned.

"I know how to hang paper. I've done it lots of times."

"Yeah, but this stuff seems different."

I unrolled a length and held it to the wall. "Isn't it

114

gorgeous! Get out of my way, Honey. I want to get started."

He shrugged and went into the living room to watch TV.

I filled a plastic trough with water and placed it on the floor beneath the place I would hang my first piece. Rolling out the paper on the carpet in the living room, I whacked off a length. Humming, I rolled it up, placed it in the water and wiggled it around a bit, then pulled it up and stuck it on the wall. With professional flair, I used the wallpaper brush to smooth it and work out air bubbles. "It's beautiful," I called out. "Come see."

By the time I had hung the second piece, the first piece had begun to crinkle and curl away from the wall. Alarmed, I pulled it back and tore it in two. "Rats," I murmured. I glanced in at Joe, then yanked it all off, wadded it up, and stuffed it in the trash compactor. Quickly I pulled off the second piece and stuck it where the first had been. By the time I was ready to hang the next piece, it also was beginning to crinkle. "Joe! Something's wrong with this paper!"

During a commercial he sauntered in. I pointed at a big wrinkle. "No matter how hard I brush it, it wrinkles. Look at that—and now this one is beginning to do it."

Joe took the brush out of my hand and began to work and work and work. Finally the two pieces seemed to be up, and reasonably smooth, but they showed signs of battle and threatened to wrinkle.

"Do you think we ought to go on?" I asked, about to cry.

"We? This is your project." He went to the trash and took out the instructions. "For best results," he read aloud, "paper must soak at least one minute before hanging." He leaned against the counter with folded arms. "There's your problem, Babe. You're in too much of a hurry." He went back to TV, and I silently continued to hang paper. Never, in all my experience, have I seen such stubborn, hateful, paper. Even after soaking each roll the right amount of time, it refused to behave. It tore, it stretched, it sagged, it bulged.

I think Joe sensed my discouragement when I threw the papering brush across the kitchen. He strolled in, picked up the brush, and took me by the hand. "Get a cup of coffee. I'll see what I can do with this last wall."

I sat at the table and watched with awe. Hadn't he said himself that he wasn't good at hanging paper? But it went up without a hitch—beautiful, smooth, no wrinkles, bubbles, or tears. Why? *How?* I didn't say a word, but my thoughts were dark. Very dark.

Woe to those who are wise in their own eyes and clever in their own sight.

Isaiah 5:21

I really should compliment Joe on a job well done. But I'm still too disgruntled.

Do not be wise in your own eyes.

Proverbs 3:7

Time Will Tell

I always said that I'd never be an old fuddy-duddy, set in my ways. I was always going to be modern, never looking back to the "good old days." But my true self has grumbled forth because of digital watches and clocks.

Two years ago our faithful alarm clock finally wore out and we replaced it with a solid state (whatever that means) clock, complete with bright red numerals we can see without our glasses, and eight buttons across the top, including snooze alarm.

Joe set it, and I was pleased with it until I had to change the alarm for an early appointment. Full directions for setting are printed on the bottom of the clock in letters that no one can see without a magnifying glass. I finally thought that I'd figured out how to change the alarm, but it was only thanks to the noisy garbage truck that I awoke in time.

That was two years ago, and I still have trouble setting it. I don't like digital watches, either. Joe was the first in our family to buy one. Apparently it was no trouble at all for him to master the four little buttons that

117

controlled days, hours, minutes, and the alarm. He liked that watch so much that he bought me a petite gold-color digital. When I tried to set it, no matter how carefully I read the directions I could not get the thing to run. The buttons had to be pushed twice, and then zeros would appear. Pushed again, numbers from one to nine would start flipping by. Pushed once more, it would go back to blinking zeros. Push the other button, the contrary thing would go blank. In desperation I handed it to Joe. Within seconds he had my watch displaying the time, and it ran accurately until the battery wore out. Fortunately, we could never find another battery for it.

Our digital clock on the VCR is also a mystery to me. The green numbers blink incessantly. It doesn't bother anyone else, but it drives me crazy. Since I can't figure out how to set it, I have taped a piece of paper over it. Even so, I can still see the blinking green.

My niece, Phyllis, came to visit from Colorado a while back, and gave me the nicest gift—my brother Charley's Hamilton pocket watch—a beautiful gold timepiece. It can be set with the stem and has glossy black numerals on its white face, with a tiny second hand that goes around. When I hold it to my ear, I can hear it, *tick-tick-tick-tick-tick-tick!* I guess I'm not as modern as I'd like to be, because I think it's the best timepiece we have.

You have made my days a mere handbreadth;
the span of my years is as nothing before you.
Each man's life is but a breath.

Psalm 39:5

Maybe I ought to study those directions again — I'd hate for the grandkids to know I can't set the VCR clock.

Now is the time of God's favor, now is the day of salvation.

2 Corinthians 6:2

Black-and-White Kitty

Since the weather is so warm, Sam and Josephine have been sleeping in the garage. Every night before we go to bed, I fill their bowls full of dry food, but every morning, although the bowls are empty, they seem to be starving. "You know what I think, Honey?" I said this morning. "I think that old black-and-white tomcat across the street sneaks in here and eats their food."

From the day we moved here that arrogant old tom has made our property part of his nightly visits. Evidently, the people who had lived here before didn't mind his mooching and they may have even fed him. At any rate, the old sourpuss seems to think our garage, as well as the whole block, belongs to him. He is big enough and strong enough to keep Sam and Josephine intimidated.

"I'm tired of his eating their food," I complained, as I put more food in the dishes. "Can't you figure some way to outsmart him?"

Joe's eyes gleamed. He loves a challenge. "I'll think of something."

After a while he called me out to look at his contraption. He had installed a coil spring to the walk-in

120

garage door, propped it open with a stick with a cord attached to it. The cord ended inside our bedroom window. "The door will only be open a few inches, but when the cat goes in, then I'll yank the cord and Mr. Tom will be trapped inside."

"Then what? How will you catch him, and what will you do with him?"

"I won't try to catch him. Cats are terrified of noise, so I'll step in the garage, bang something, yell, holler, and chase him around. When I figure he's had enough, I'll open the door." He grinned confidently. "I'll guarantee you, he'll never come back."

It sounded pretty good to me, so when it got dark I put Sam and Josephine in the house, and Joe and I went to the bedroom to wait.

After a while our eyes got used to the dark, and then we saw the black-and-white cat slip into the garage. *BANG!* went the door as Joe yanked the cord. "I got him!" He grabbed a big metal mixing bowl and a wooden spoon and rushed outside. Cautiously, he slipped his hand inside the garage to flip on the light, then opened the door a little wider.

"Oh, no!" He backed out and slammed the door. "It's a skunk!"

He opened the double door that faces the street and we both waited, wondering what we'd do if the skunk decided to take up residence. After about thirty minutes Mr. Skunk walked out and disappeared into the night. But not until he'd eaten all the cat food.

Look at the birds of the air; they do not sow or reap or store away in barns, and yet your heavenly Father feeds them. Are you not much more valuable than they?

Matthew 6:26

We still don't know if the skunk or the cat has been eating our cats' food, but one thing we know, the Lord takes care of "critters."

But this happened that we might not rely on ourselves but on God.

2 Corinthians 1:9

Sidetracked

We were getting ready for church when I noticed Joe riffling through his shirts. "Which one are you looking for?"

"The tan-and-white striped."

"Whoops!" I dropped the hairbrush and hurried to the back bedroom. There his shirt was—on the ironing board where I'd left it yesterday afternoon—and the iron was still on.

What was the matter with me? How could I have forgotten that yesterday I was ironing? I remembered that while I was ironing, the mail came with a past-due telephone bill. The payment had to be made that very day or service would be cut off, so I had scribbled the check and dashed to the postal substation. Unfortunately, they also have greeting cards there, and I remembered that my granddaughter Jeni's birthday was coming up. I probably spent an hour there, looking at cards. When I came back home, I noticed that crabgrass had practically taken over the rose garden, so I worked on that a while. When I came in, it was time to start making dinner, so with all thoughts of ironing completely gone I got busy in the kitchen.

Joe called, "I can wear something else. We're going to be late."

"I'll be done in a jiffy," I yelled back, ironing as fast as I could. (At least I didn't have to wait for the iron to heat.) How much money does it cost to heat an iron for twenty hours? I could have set the house on fire! What was it going to take to change me from a scatterbrain to a sensible person, one who can concentrate on and finish a job? Just last week I was trying to compose a business letter and wasn't sure how to spell "cursory," so I opened the dictionary to the "C" section and began to read the definitions for *cudbear, cui bono, cuirassier, curculio, currycomb*—fascinating! I spent almost half an hour reading before I finally got back to writing the letter. By then my train of thought was gone, and so was the mail.

Joe did a bit of sputtering while he buttoned his shirt, mentioning that it would be nice to be early sometimes and how he hates to walk in after everyone else is seated. I sort of promised him that it wouldn't happen again.

The wisdom of the prudent is to give thought to their ways.

Proverbs 14:8

All through church I was miserable — not so much because I'd made us late but because I couldn't remember — had I, or had I not turned off the iron?

Therefore, my dear brothers, stand firm. Let nothing move you. Always give yourselves fully to the work of the Lord, because you know that your labor in the Lord is not in vain.

1 Corinthians 15:58

124

Saving Big

Joe and I are members of Discount Warehouse, a gigantic store where the savings on big items, such as TVs, refrigerators, and washing machines, are considerable. We shop there about once a week and have figured out that we can save anywhere from twenty cents to a dollar on most grocery and household items. The catch is you have to buy in quantity. Before joining, one ought to ask oneself how long it will take, for example, to use twelve twenty-ounce jars of mustard. It's been three years ago this summer since we bought our twelve bottles. We've used two; four are still in the cupboard; and I've given away the other six. That's what we usually wind up doing with a lot of the stuff. I share it with the kids or neighbors, which is nice, but we would probably be ahead if we bypassed Discount and shopped at the most expensive market in town. Sadly, I've even had to throw out some perishable items such as bread, mayonnaise, and margarine. Who can use a gallon of mayonnaise before it's rancid?

Once I went with Joe's sister and we divided a few items. That's the way to do it, provided that you can shop with someone who likes the same things you like. Patti can't stand anything with cheese in it, so a five-pound chunk of cheddar was out. We couldn't share a huge box of green pasta because Joe wouldn't touch it. We couldn't share a case of cat or dog food, because she has a dog and we have cats; therefore, about the only thing we could share was some bread and a twelve-pack of women's ankle socks.

Besides buying in quantity, another drawback to shopping at Discount is that everything is such a fantastic bargain that you keep piling your cart with stuff. Almost every week we buy at least one big bunch of something we don't need. At the moment, we have toilet tissue, Kleenex, and paper towels stored in both bathrooms and the kitchen cupboard. The freezer compartment is stuffed with twenty-four pack chicken thighs and drumsticks, fifty-pack ground beef patties, two-pack English muffins, and bagels.

It's so full that there is no room for ice cubes or ice cream. The refrigerator is packed, too. At Discount, cranberry juice, orange juice, and canola oil all come in gallon jugs, so I have had to pour them into various sizes of Tupperware and jars and stick them wherever I could. At the bottom of the fridge a half-gallon jug of dill pickles is always in my way, and a humongous bottle of salad dressing takes up most of the lower shelf.

On wash day I have to wrestle with a carton of Tide so big that a dog could sleep in it, and I'm sure I have enough Simple Green, Windex, Soft Soap, and floor wax to last the rest of my life.

The last time we were there, I wrote a check for $109.90. I shook my head in dismay. "But—think of the money we saved," I said.

Joe struggled to push the basket to the car. He rested a minute, then said, "I'm not sure I can afford to save all this money."

In the house of the wise are stores of choice food and oil, but a foolish man devours all he has.

Proverbs 21:20

I wish I knew for sure if we were saving or losing!

When they had all had enough to eat, he said to his disciples, "Gather the pieces that are left over. Let nothing be wasted."

John 6:12

Better Than You

When I'm driving and Joe is with me, I get the distinct impression that he doesn't have a lot of confidence in my ability. He says things like, "Watch it!" — "You're too close to the curb" — and "You'd better get in the left lane now," but it's not so much what he says as his attitude. I take my turn driving so he can rest, but he's about as relaxed as a deer in hunting season. He sits up straight, twitches a lot, presses his foot on the floor, and never takes his eyes off the road. They glance to and fro, watching for any possible hazard. Just knowing how closely he watches, makes me do stupid things. Conversely, when *he's* driving I'm completely at ease. I've balanced the check book (within a dollar or so), written thank-you notes, done my nails, even slipped out of dress clothes into sweats when he's at the wheel. But when I'm driving—instead of resting, his pulse is racing.

His lack of trust in my ability isn't fair. I learned to drive a boyfriend's car when I was fifteen—actually, I almost learned sooner than that, because my Uncle George used to let me sit on his lap and steer and shift gears in his old Packard when I was only seven. I've been

128

chauffering kids and relatives around forever. So why doesn't Joe trust me?

True, I had a couple of near-misses on our latest trip, owing to looking at the scenery and sky, but we didn't run off the road or hit anybody, so what's the big deal? And I can drive in city traffic as well as he can. They say Los Angeles drivers are the best drivers in the world because we have to be—to stay alive.

"Other cities may not have the same rules," Joe warned, but I just told him, that's their problem. I mean, if they want to poke along at twenty-five, then they can expect to be honked at, or passed even if the traffic lanes are narrow.

If Joe weren't so good to me, I might call him a male chauvinist because he thinks my driving skills are inferior to his. However, when I think of last summer when he maneuvered our twenty-seven foot motor home up, up, up, over and down a single-lane, twisting-and-turning pass, I have to concede he's a good mountain driver. No wonder. He used to drive a tank truck. It could be that his driving skill is just a tad better than mine. It's possible.

Do you see a man wise in his own eyes? There is more hope for a fool than for him.

Proverbs 26:12

Of course, if Joe had fainted, I'm sure I could have driven that mountain pass.

The man who thinks he knows something does not yet know as he ought to know.

1 Corinthians 8:2

129

On Their Appointed Rounds

Neither snow nor rain
Nor heat, nor gloom of night
Stays these couriers
From the swift completion
Of their appointed rounds.

I read somewhere that this is the inscription on the main post office in New York City. I'm sure the first part of the message is true—but it doesn't mean that these couriers can't change their schedules. Ray, our postman, has always been as reliable as the sunrise. Every day for two years except holidays, at exactly eleven-thirty he drives up in a funny looking white van with red, white, and blue stripes, stops at our curbside mailbox, and fills it will bills, junk mail, and an occasional letter. He is so dependable that I know it's time to start making lunch when he gets to our house. I also know that if I want to get mail picked up, I have until eleven twenty-five to get it out in the box.

Yesterday morning I was paying bills, some of which were due that day, so I was rushing to get them out in the mailbox. I scribbled checks, addressed envelopes, and

130

watched the clock. At eleven twenty-five I jumped up, still licking the last stamp, grabbed the envelopes, and loped outside.

As I yanked open the mailbox, an ad fell out, then some more pieces. The box was already full of junk mail. "Double-crosser!" I whispered. I looked up and down the street. Not a sign of Ray or his stupid van. How had he come by without my seeing him? As I was picking up the junk mail, Chloë came trotting out of her house.

"Did you notice what time the mailman came by?" I asked.

"Yeah." She shoved the last of a doughnut in her mouth. "He was here about eight-thirty."

"Of all the nerve," I griped to Joe. "Changing schedules! Whoever heard of the mail coming at eight-thirty in the morning? Now one of us is going to have to drive to the post office and mail these bills!"

"Just put 'em in the box," Joe suggested. "If he picks the mail up that early, we probably won't have to pay late charges."

This morning we were both at the window at eight-thirty, looking for Ray. Eight-forty-five, nine o'clock, and still not a sign of him.

I bit my lip. "Maybe you'd better take the bills to the post office."

Joe sighed and reached for his jacket. "You're probably right."

"I think the mail service is going down the tubes," I snorted.

This afternoon at *four-thirty* the mail truck stopped out front. With arms folded across my chest, I marched out to ask Ray why he was so late. A shapely young

131

woman in blue shorts smiled at me. "Where's our regular mailman?" I asked.

"Ray?" She flipped her long hair back. "He's transferred to another route. I'll be delivering your mail, at least today. Who knows about tomorrow?" She laughed as she drove away.

"Hmm," Joe grunted, leaning against the porch. "I think the mail service is improving."

Do not boast about tomorrow, for you do not know what a day may bring forth.

Proverbs 27:1

I'm not the least bit jealous of that cute mail person. I'm just upset about the schedule always changing.

Why, you do not even know what will happen tomorrow. What is your life? You are a mist that appears for a little while and then vanishes.

James 4:14

Nothing New

From the time our oldest grandson Danny was a toddler, he loved music. Some of his first crayon drawings were of his record player and records. While other tykes his age were scuffling outside with their puppies and friends, Danny was listening to music, or pounding on the piano. When he was seven, he began to take piano lessons. Now I know I sound like a typical grandmother, but he was very good. I loved watching his little fingers pound out Beethoven and Bach. In junior high he took up trumpet, and I thought he was very, very good. In high school he went crazy over jazz and improvisation. Whether on trumpet or piano, he played strange melodies for hours. He also organized a jazz band, which evidently was pretty good, because people actually paid for their services.

At a recent family gathering Danny announced, "I've decided that this year I'm going to become a *monster!*"

Appalled, I cried, "Danny! What do you mean?"

He and brother David, who is following in Danny's musical footsteps, both stared, then began to laugh at me. "Grandmother, *monster* just means *the best* in music. I'm going to practice and practice until I'm the best."

"On trumpet? Piano?"

"No. Bass." He strummed with his fingers on his stomach.

David began to drum on the table. "Yeah!" He jumped up. "I gotta go emcee now."

I looked at David. "You'll make a good emcee."

Again these two smart-aleck grandsons laughed at me.

"*Emcee* means jam, Grandmother." When I frowned, David looked knowingly at Danny.

Danny smiled kindly. "'Jam' is when musicians get together and play."

"I knew that!" I glared at him. "Do you think I'm a dock?"

"You mean *dork*," David corrected. "A sideshow freak."

"Geek," Danny added. "Well, I'd better get going, too. I may end up as a joke."

"Joke?"

"Loser."

The boys exchanged looks, then said good-bye.

Next time I'm with those musicians, I think I'll try a little of my vocabulary and see how they like it. Instead of "monster," I'll lay *hepcat, smoothie,* and *lollapaloosa* on them, and for "dork," I'll stun them with *twerp, fathead,* or *goofball.* As for "joke"—how about *kaput?*

What has been will be again, what has been done will be done again; there is nothing new under the sun.

Ecclesiastes 1:9

134

I hate *not being with it. I'd better listen to some of those goofy radio stations and learn their lingo.*

Is there anything of which one can say, "Look! This is something new"?

Ecclesiastes 1:10

The Unobservers

We haven't been with Marian and Fred for almost a year; in fact, the last time they came to our house, Joe hadn't started remodeling the kitchen.

When she called and said they would be out in about an hour, I went into my usual frantic "people-are-coming" routine. I plowed through the rooms, kicking magazines under the couch and flinging clothes at the closets. I was out of breath when I went to the kitchen.

"Thank heavens that I won't have to do much in here," I said to Joe. "I can't wait for Marian to see it."

When they drove up, we went out to meet them, and I drew Marian right into the kitchen. "I'll put on coffee," I said, letting my hand linger on the new counter while the other pointed gracefully toward the cupboards.

She flopped in a chair. "Fred and I have been looking at new homes out in Riverside, and oh, you should see the *kitchens*! The style now is white or pastel cupboards—not dark old things like yours and mine!"

My mouth fell open. Couldn't she see how much lighter my cupboards were? Hadn't she even noticed the new sink? The counters? The extra room in the kitchen?

In the living room I heard Fred ask, "Well, what have you been doing lately?"

"Not much," Joe answered. "Did a little remodeling in the kitchen."

"I just built a patio," Fred said. "Worked like a dog on that sucker. Now *she's* talking about moving." For the next fifteen minutes Fred talked about lumber, concrete, and aching muscles, while Marian kept raving about new homes. Neither one said a word about our kitchen.

After I poured coffee, Fred said, "Joe, you didn't see what we drove up in. Did you?"

Joe stood up and looked out the window. "Well I'll be—a brand new Chevy."

"I can't believe you didn't see it when we drove up!" Marian looked reproachful. "You two are really unobservant."

My eyebrows shot up. "*We* are unobservant! Neither one of you noticed all the work we've done in our kitchen!"

Marian and Fred looked around the kitchen. "It's beautiful," Marian said. "I feel terrible for not noticing it," and Fred nodded contritely.

"I'm sorry we didn't notice the car," Joe said. "I guess we're all too wrapped up in ourselves."

Each of you should look not only to your own interests, but also to the interests of others.

Philippians 2:4

I still think — well, all cars look alike — but our kitchen is one-of-a-kind!

But God has combined the members of the body ... so that there should be no division in the body, but that its parts should have equal concern for each other.

1 Corinthians 12:24–25

Hanging Pictures

When Joe and I were newlyweds, it seemed to me that he thought of me as being perfect. No matter what I did, he said it was fine. Every accomplishment, from blobby oil paintings to lumpy ceramics was something for him to brag on. He loved my family, liked my friends, even made a scratching post for my cat, so it was a real surprise after we moved into our first home when he found fault with the way I was hanging pictures. My method is to put the pictures on the floor the way I want them, then hang them on the wall. (It's practically foolproof, although I usually have to take the nails out for each picture and move them around a few times.)

That day, I'd been hammering then pulling out nails for quite a while when he strode into the room and took the hammer out of my hand.

"In the first place," he said, "you don't use three-inch nails."

"Joe, I know from experience that if I don't use these long nails they fall out of the plaster."

"That's why you use these." He showed me some short nails with brass hooks attached. "Now, what do you want hung, and where?"

139

"I already have that one of the blue bonnets where I want it, so—"

"I'll re-hang it with one of these." He lifted the painting off the three-inch nail and saw five holes in the wall. "What did you use, a rake?"

"Every time I hung it, it wasn't quite where I wanted it."

"Did you ever think of using a tape measure?" His voice was downright testy. "Now before we can hang anything, I've got to plaster these holes."

"Oh, Joe. That's ridiculous! Nobody can see them. We'll be here all day if you keep on finding fault with every little old thing."

It was evening before we finally had all the pictures hung. And that was the day I realized he didn't think I am completely perfect. It was also the day I realized what a hang-up he has about holes in the walls. "Promise me," he said, looking deep into my eyes, "—the next time you want to hang pictures, you'll let me do it."

I didn't promise, and since then we've lived in several other houses with inviting bare walls on which I am very careful to hang pictures when he is away from home. If he only knew how many times I have changed pictures around and left holes in the walls, he'd probably have a heart attack. But I am very sly. If my arrangement doesn't cover the holes, I mix up a paste of Wilhold glue and bath powder, and stuff it in with a knife. It's every bit as good as plaster and smells better, too.

When Joe brought in the mail today, we received some new pictures of the grandkids. Feeling a little guilty for the years of fooling Joe, I said, "Oh, look at these new pictures. Would you be kind enough to hang them for me?"

He was silent for so long that I wondered if he had heard me; then he gave me his sly fox grin. "I imagine you can do it just fine without any help from me. You've been doing it for years."

You may be sure that your sin will find you out.
Numbers 32:23

I can't believe he's known all these years and didn't say anything. What a deceitful person!

Though I taught them again and again, they would not listen or respond to discipline.
Jeremiah 32:33

Heat Wave

We're having a heat wave. Every day the temperature soars to 100 degrees in the shade, and some days it's even gone to 105 degrees. Joe and I have been spending a lot of time in the pool. What a refuge—and it's fun, too. However, as the weather gets hotter, the pool becomes the source of a few problems.

Number one problem: ALGAE. Tiny monster plants somehow invade the water unnoticed, then suddenly take over, changing the sparkling blue to a goopy green. The slimy stuff builds up between the tiles and along the bottom and sides. Once it starts, it takes Joe two days of hard work, and costs several dollars for chemicals to get the pool sparkling again.

Number two problem: PALM TREE SEEDS. Jim and Larita, our neighbors behind us, have seven stately palms. When I'm sunbathing by the pool, I can look up at these lovely trees and pretend I'm in Hawaii. But hot weather causes hundreds—yea, thousands—of little palm seed-bearing parachutes to be released in the air. These little crafts hover over our property, then drop in the pool like little paratroopers invading. They clog up

142

the filters, are disgusting to swim in, and cause Joe to mutter and complain a *lot*.

Number three problem: KIDS. Having raised our own, we know how fun it is for kids of all ages to get to go swimming, especially on hot days. Can we deny our neighbors' kids this privilege? Can we enjoy playing around in the water like a couple of comfortable old seals while they're sweltering? I've tried, but I can't forget those sweat-streaked little faces, those listless bodies, with no cool place to play.

We invite the ones who live closest to come on in. That's Chris and Kim, and their friends sometimes, and Anthony, Stacie, and Nathan. They come with their radios, snacks, drinks, and towels. The pool becomes alive with kids diving, jumping, yelling, and some even swim. The water gets too turbulent for me, so I stay out of their way. Joe sits in a deck chair, his old straw hat jauntily over his eyes, and although each one can swim, he constantly watches for trouble. I watch, too, wishing I could look like Chris and Kim in their bikinis . . .

These are the three pool problems brought on by the heat wave, but the good side is that the kids get the water churning so hard it helps keep the algae down. Too, Larita has realized what a nuisance the palm tree seeds are and has come over every day for a week to help clean the pool. As for the kids, they think we're pretty nice. The girls, Chris, Kim, and Stacie, always give us a hug and kiss. Anthony and Nathan give us five.

Jesus replied ". . . 'love your neighbor as yourself.'"

Matthew 19:18

143

Joe says sometimes he'd like to fill in the pool. Maybe it's a good idea — except we'd miss the kids.

Nobody should seek his own good, but the good of others.

1 Corinthians 10:24

Not My Fault

Joe and I were at LAX to meet friends. Because their flight was delayed, we went to one of the coffee shops to kill time. We took seats at a counter facing the windows so we could watch the planes landing and taking off.

"Isn't this exciting?" I squeezed his arm. "I'd rather sit here and see the planes than be at one of the tables." I glanced behind me where a narrow aisle separated the counter stool from a row of tables. Five people were seated at the table directly behind me, and the man at the end had evidently pulled up an extra chair because he was partway in the aisle. I saw a woman coming toward us, loaded down with a big bag on one shoulder, a camera swinging from her other shoulder, and carrying a full tray of food.

I had just turned my attention back to the action on the runways when I felt something touch my neck. I looked up in time to see the loaded-down woman lift her tray up above the man's head, which caused her shoulder bag to catch on the back of my chair. As though the scene were in slow motion, I saw her tugging forward, tray held high, camera swinging from side to side, but unable to move as long as she was tethered by her shoulder bag. In a flash of understanding, I lifted her bag and she was free. However, the sudden shift of weight made her lose her balance, the tray tipped, and most of a large Coke spilled on the poor man's head and shoulders.

"YEOW!" he howled, leaping to his feet, and swiping wildly at his head and shoulders.

"Oh! Oh!" the woman moaned. "I'm so terribly sorry! I don't know how that happened!"

I turned quickly and stared out the window.

"What happened?" Joe whispered.

I shrugged. "Evidently the woman spilled her drink on the man."

"I can see that," he grated. "But how did it happen?"

"How should I know?" I had to look away from his piercing stare. "Accidents happen."

"Especially around you." He continued to eye me.

"Joe! Trust me! It wasn't my fault!"

Not exactly.

Do not steal. Do not lie. Do not deceive one another.

Leviticus 19:11

If I hadn't helped her, she might have spilled the Coke on me!

Friend deceives friend, and no one speaks the truth.

Jeremiah 9:5

Dining Table

I don't know how it is at your house, but our dining table is a big brown magnet. It draws everything to it—library books, my purse, the groceries, and especially the mail. I've always admired homemakers who keep an empty, shining, dining table with only a bouquet of flowers or a lovely plant to decorate it. You'd think, as hard as both of us have worked on the kitchen-dinette area, that we'd make an effort to keep it neat. I've tried, but table-piling must be in our genes. The dining table wherever we've lived has always been the hub of activity. Even before the kids left home, I would periodically have a fit over the messy table and would threaten the family with instant pain if *anybody* put so much as a paperclip on the table. Everyone would be careful for a few days, but something would come up to break down my vigilance. Income tax would have to be prepared, or some ongoing project at school would have to be done on the table. Before long, the table would be covered again. And I admit, part of the mess usually included some of my hobbies.

Now that it's just Joe and I, you'd think we could

keep the table clear. Barbara gave me a beautiful basket of silk flowers I use as a centerpiece, but right now you can barely see the flowers because the daily paper is spread out over them.

Yesterday's ads and flyers are still scattered around, as well as the ever-present *Reader's Digest* sweepstakes letter and accompanying mystery stamps. Joe hasn't taken time to figure out what he's supposed to send in. I don't know why he even wastes his time, but he always says, "You can't win if you don't send it back."

I'm just as bad. Coupons from Blair and Carol Wright have been on the table for two days because I can't decide whether or not they're worth using. And I keep knocking over two empty prescription bottles on the table because I keep forgetting to order refills.

I don't know how to solve this problem. One day I took a sheet of typing paper and with a marking pen scrawled, "Do Not Put Anything On This Table." Joe came in with the mail, reading as he walked, and dropped a couple of magazines on top of my note. I'm not sure if he saw the note or not. I've thought about putting blocks under the legs on one side so that everything would slide off, but then I'd just have to pick it up. What I need is a magnet in reverse, a repellent, so that as soon as you try to put something down it will fly right back into your hand.

One who is slack in his work is brother to one who destroys.

Proverbs 18:9

I could take the table out, and put the mail directly in the trash.

We do not want you to become lazy.

Hebrews 6:12

Garage Sale

"Joan just called." I stood in the garage doorway and watched Joe take the lawn mower's carburetor apart, which he does quite often. He bought the old thing at a garage sale and he's determined to make it work.

"Yeh? What'd she want?"

"She and Don are going to have a garage sale and wondered if we wanted to bring anything over." I looked around at our garage. "Couldn't we get rid of some of this stuff? We could make some extra money."

"I don't want to get rid of any of mine. I use all these tools."

"Six hammers?"

"Why don't you sell those frames?"

"No. I might get back into oil painting again." I wandered over to a dusty piece of machinery. "How long has it been since you used this thing?"

He looked at it. "My lathe? A while. But I may use it tomorrow."

"How about that little electric heater up there on the shelf? We could sell that."

"Nope. Once in a while during cold weather, I use it while I'm working out here."

I wandered around, peeking under plastic covers, moving a few things, snooping. "We never play darts anymore. We could probably get a couple of dollars for that board."

"We couldn't sell it. Darts have been outlawed."

"Did you know you have five saws? We could sell some of those."

"Hey. We're not selling my stuff. If you want to sell something, how about your typewriters? You have at least four that I know of."

"My typewriters! Are you crazy? The portable was made in 1926! And the Underwood in 1931, and the Royal in 1940. I'm not about to part with those antiques."

I looked around some more. Every wall was covered with trash that men hold dear. "Don't you have three lawn mowers, not counting that piece of junk?"

I saw a dangerous flash in his eyes. "Two lawn mowers," he said quietly. "The other machine is an edger."

"How about this wheelbarrow?"

"Let's go in and have some coffee. Then maybe we can see if we can't get rid of some of your junk."

I knew I was whipped. He'll never part with his treasures. And I'm not about to let him paw through my valuables.

In everything, do to others what you would have them do to you, for this sums up the Law and the Prophets.

Matthew 7:12

150

Maybe I could sneak some of his things over to Joan's. He'd never miss them.

Honor one another above yourselves.
Romans 12:10

151

No Sew

When the leaves start turning and the air feels crisp, I always get an urge to buy patterns and materials. I realized a long time ago that I was not a seamstress. When the kids were little, I tried. Two of my best friends just *loved* to sew, or so they said, and both encouraged me.

"You'll save so much money!" Millie promised.

"Look at this outfit," chimed in Rhea, stunning in a pink suit. "I made it from a remnant that only cost a dollar sixty-nine." That year, enticed by dreams of how well dressed we would look and how much money we would save, I spent enough on patterns and material to buy each of us a new wardrobe.

My poor kids. They had to wear dresses and shirts that were so peculiar. Hemlines sagged in places and rose in others. Buttonhole stitching looked like false eyelashes. The flap that conceals the zipper on skirts and trousers never stayed flat. Little dresses often had to have a tuck pinned in at the last moment, or a bow attached to cover a mistake. I remember a green dress I made for myself that, for some reason I could never figure out, had an extra amount of material dropping on one side. It looked as though it had been stretched by a basketball. I wore it but was always careful to hold my purse over that drape.

When Nicole was about two, I broke my vow never to sew again, and bought doll patterns to make clothes for her dolls. *Doll clothes should be easy*, I reasoned, but, to my dismay, the patterns were just as hard to follow as they had been for real clothes thirty years ago. Directions like, "Put single notches together, with outside edge of B matching inside edge of C, folded in the center" drive me crazy. I did make some doll clothes that year, but instead of fitting her sixteen-inch baby doll, I could barely get them on Chrystal's Barbie doll.

As the years go by, it makes me sad that I have never made things for the grandchildren. Other grandmothers knit afghans, make little suits and dresses, embroider darling yokes for baby dresses, but I know my limitations. I can play games with them, or draw pictures for them, go on walks with them, read Bible stories—but sadly, they'll have no keepsake fancy pillows, shawls, or crocheted tablecloths from me.

Each one should use whatever gift he has received to serve others, faithfully administering God's grace in its various forms.

1 Peter 4:10

Wonder if I should take a sewing class? Maybe I could make something charming for the grandkids. Probably, though, I'd better tackle that stack of mending that's been in a box for two years.

In everything set them an example by doing what is good.

Titus 2:7

Care Circle

"I'll be glad to have Care Circle at our house next time," I said to Barbara, our Bible study leader. I love our Care Circle, and at that insane moment I really wanted them to come to our house, but from the moment I volunteered I began to worry. I would have to clean house and serve refreshments. I began to feel weak, and broke out in a sweat.

Barbara looked startled. "Are you okay?"

"Fine," I whispered.

On the way home Joe said, "You're already worrying, aren't you?" At a red light, he looked at me. "Why do you get so upset? These people are our *friends*. Friends accept you the way you are, or else they aren't friends."

He just didn't understand. Friends or not, I couldn't stand for them to see our house. For the next two weeks all my energies were focused on *the meeting* as though I was seeing our home for the first time. The hood over the stove had a film of grease and fuzz. The top of the refrigerator was piled high with magazines and papers. The front room drapes looked exhausted. Cobwebs floated from the corners. The bathrooms—revolting.

How could I have my friends come to this disgusting place? Over the next ten days, though, driven by fear of discovery, the house began to look presentable.

Meanwhile, every day I tried to decide what to serve. For some women that wouldn't present a problem, but I've had so many cooking failures: angel food cakes that refused to rise; pies with unchewable crust; chocolate mousse with the consistency of hot chocolate. I can't even cook prepared cookie dough without burning it. I don't have a lot of confidence in my cooking. I finally decided to buy frozen pies. If they didn't turn out right, I could blame Mrs. Smith.

The day before the meeting I tackled our bathrooms. Armed with rubber gloves, Ajax, Fantastic, and Sani-Flush, I worked about fifteen minutes on Joe's bathroom, and at least an hour on mine. "No one ever uses your bathroom," I explained to Joe, "so I don't have to clean too much in there." That afternoon I bought a new bathmat set, towels, and a plant to dress up my sparkling bathroom. I made Joe promise that he wouldn't go in there, because I didn't want footprints on the new rug. The day of the meeting, my insides felt quivery, and I kept finding things out of place or something I forgot to dust. About five in the afternoon Joe said, "When are we going to eat?"

"Eat? I'm not about to mess up the kitchen. And I don't want cooking smells in the house! We can get a sandwich at Carl Jr.'s."

That night after everyone went home, Joe said, "It was a good Bible study."

"Mmm."

"It was a good prayer time, too."

"Mmm."

"The pies were eaten. They drank your coffee." I didn't answer. "What's the matter? You don't seem happy."

"Not one person went in my bathroom!" I exploded. "I did all that work, bought a new mat, and towels, and a plant! All for nothing!"

"That's not so bad, is it?"

"Of course it's bad! They used *your* bathroom!"

But Martha (Mab) was distracted by all the preparations that had to be made.

Luke 10:40

I didn't remember anything about the Bible study — I was too worried about what people thought of Joe's bathroom.

They devoted themselves to the apostles' teaching and to the fellowship, to the breaking of bread and to prayer.

Acts 2:42

Awana

"Do you believe the Lord wants little children to know the word of God?" Marilyn, the director of AWANA, stood at the pulpit, making her yearly plea for helpers in AWANA, an international youth association. "Besides having fun and learning crafts," she went on, "all our kids memorize Scripture. In fact, that's what the word AWANA stands for—'Approved Workmen Are Not Ashamed.' If you believe the Lord meant it when He said, 'Let the little children come to me,' then please come help us on Wednesday nights." She smiled wistfully. "We really need you to keep this work going. Grandparents, you could help by listening to the kids recite their memorized Bible verses."

On the way home from church Joe said, "I think we ought to help out on Wednesdays."

I stared at him in surprise. "But we couldn't go to Pastor Bob's Bible study."

"That's true, but I think the kids need us."

Next Wednesday night we were at church, but instead of going to the classroom for Bible study, we went to the main entrance. The whole area from the front to the back parking lot was teeming with kids, like a gigantic anthill that someone had kicked open. Big kids in a huge circle were screaming their heads off over some game; smaller kids wiggled around a sign-up desk; a group of preteen girls were dancing, prancing, and turning cartwheels on the lawn. A few toddlers cried inconsolably as parents left them with harried helpers.

As I took in the scene, a feeling of desperation swept over me. "Let's get out of here," I whispered, turning back toward our car.

"Come on," Joe urged. "Marilyn said that all we have to do is listen to the kids say verses."

As we searched for Marilyn through chilly rooms, we passed a group of Cubbies doing crafts. The little cuties were trying to glue plastic eyes and felt noses on chenille snakes. All had glue in varying amounts on their clothes, hands, and faces. One cherub had glued a felt ball to her own nose. The leader, a recent bride, seemed stunned and helpless as we walked on by.

When we found Marilyn, she assigned Joe to help with the "Pals," a group of nine-year-old boys. She took me to the "Sparks"—kindergarten kids who seemed determined to either kick each other, throw crayons, or climb over chairs.

Driving home after that first Wednesday, we were silent. I don't know about Joe, but I was exhausted and in shock over our commitment. We'd promised Marilyn nine months!

At home, with a cup of hot chocolate, Joe said dreamily, "It was hard, but they were nice kids. I'm looking forward to next Wednesday."

I rolled my eyes up. Lord, help me! Next Wednesday I would have to help that darling Danny say, ". . . the

Father thent the Thon to be the Thavior of the world." I would probably have to let that cuddly Marcy sit on my lap again because she was afraid of the other kids. Maybe little Ricky would fight to sit by me like he did tonight. Oh, well. It's just one night a week.

> Let the little children come to me, and do not hinder them.
>
> Mark 10:14

What amazed me is that most of those kids learned the verse, and I still can't say it.

> Do your best to present yourself to God as one approved, a workman who does not need to be ashamed and who correctly handles the word of truth.
>
> 2 Timothy 2:15

Poor Taste

I had a disgusting experience this morning. The weather has turned cold, so I decided to cook oatmeal. I was really looking forward to a big bowl of hot cereal with lots of sugar and milk, but with the first mouthful I rushed to the bathroom and spit it out! Somehow I had picked up the spoon I used to dish out the cats' tuna! Yuk! I still gag when I remember it.

Isn't it a jolt when your taste buds are set for one flavor and you eat something entirely different? Not long ago I cut a piece of cake with the same knife I had just used to slice onions. Onion-flavored chocolate is an awful shock—almost as bad as taking a big swig of sour milk. One of the worst taste disappointments I remember was when I decided to buy a gorgeous piece of Danish pastry, which turned out to be a cheese blintz. How can people eat those things? And I'll never forgive the person who said to me, "Try it! You'll like it!" as she gave me a piece of Limburger cheese.

I guess we'll never understand why some people like the taste of things that make others sick. My brother had a friend who poured syrup on pinto beans. I couldn't bear to watch him eat that mess.

160

I've been trying to figure out how I could have used that tuna spoon in my cereal this morning, and I think I've traced it down. In the past three months I've ruined four teaspoons by not realizing that they had slipped down and were hiding in the garbage disposal. Have you ever done that? Man, that horrible *clackety-clack* always startles me so much that I can't react in time to turn it off before the blades wreck the spoons.

"I know a simple solution," my smart sis said. "Never put the spoons in the sink. Either put them directly in the dishwasher or lay them on the counter."

I've been careful to do that, so this morning I must have taken a clean spoon out of the drawer for my oatmeal and placed it beside the tuna spoon. How disgusting. How disappointing! I doubt I'll ever eat oatmeal again—and definitely not tuna.

Taste and see that the Lord is good; blessed is the man who takes refuge in him.
Psalm 34:8

Recently our water has had a poor taste, sort of like iodine — disappointing when you're thirsty.

On the last and greatest day of the Feast, Jesus stood and said in a loud voice, "If a man is thirsty, let him come to me and drink."
John 7:37

The Daily Paper

We've about decided to quit taking the daily paper. I asked our paper boy if we could just take it on Sundays, but he said no—every day or not at all. If it were an evening paper, it might be different. We'd have more time to read it. But receiving a morning paper every day sure makes a big useless mess of papers to dispose of.

It would be different, too, if we really enjoyed reading it, but most of it goes unlooked at, much less read. Joe reads the first page and the sports and I read the funnies and Ann Landers. Then it's just there on the kitchen table in the way until I move it. I usually pull out all the ads and look through them every day, and Joe quite often will look through the classifieds; but for the rest of it—we have already heard it on the ten o'clock news the night before.

On the positive side, it's interesting to read local news, like when our shopping center was robbed, or a police chase raced by our house, or somebody you know might have his picture in the paper. Even Joan and Don have had their picture in the paper this last year because of school activities. And Dwight, one of the fellows in our Care Circle, had his picture in a few weeks ago with a nice article about his business. But most of the time, the newspaper is just an irritant. First I stack it on the fridge, then I carry it out to the garage, then Joe takes it out to the trash, hoping someone will pick it up. Then the wind comes up and blows papers all over. Or it rains and makes mounds of soggy sludge we have to shovel into the trash barrel. I used to save papers for my nephew, but he doesn't take part in paper drives now that he's in high school. In fact, I'm not sure there are paper drives anymore. People are always talking about recycling, but we can't find anyone interested in collecting papers.

I've definitely made up my mind, and I'm sure Joe agrees. When the paper boy comes, I'll just tell him we don't want it anymore.

Well. He came. He's a nice kid. He's had this same route for four years. We've watched him grow from a short freckle-faced kid in seventh grade to a tall, good-looking boy who plays basketball on the high school team. When I saw him, I couldn't decide whether to stop the paper or not, so I just paid him. I'll send Joe to the door next month.

> He who doubts is like a wave of the sea, blown
> and tossed by the wind.
>
> James 1:6

Maybe Joe and I could learn how to make papier-mâché masks or piñatas.

> He is a double-minded man, unstable in all he
> does.
>
> James 1:8

Looking Up

Joe and I usually take our walks together, but one day last week he wasn't feeling too well so I walked alone. Although I missed him, I was sort of glad to be by myself because he never walks as fast as I want to go. After all, if we're doing it for the aerobic benefits, we need to *move*.

It was a beautiful fall morning with no smog. The sky was postcard blue, and the leaves on the liquid-amber trees were turning reddish orange. I was strutting along, swinging my arms, breathing deeply, and looking up at the sky. *This is the way to take a walk!* Suddenly I stepped on one of the liquid-amber seed pods, which are about as hard as a golf ball. My ankle turned and I felt as though I'd been tackled. I fell hard on both hands and my right hip. My right eye was so close to the sidewalk I could see pores in the concrete. My hands and wrists felt as though they were on fire, my shoulders seemed to be jerked out of their sockets, and my hip and knees throbbed. But the worst pain of all was the humiliation.

I tried to jump right up, but it took all my strength to pull my knees up under me and slowly rock back and forth on sore legs and arms. I was sure someone had seen me and would be rushing out to see if I needed help. "Oh, no," I would say. "I'm just fine!" But nobody came. I was both relieved and worried. If my bones were broken, how could I get home?

I stood up slowly. I looked all around. Still not a soul anywhere. Were people watching behind those windows, wondering if I were drunk or on drugs? Or did they shake their heads and murmur, "Poor old lady—senile, you know."

I took a painful step, then another. Thank the Lord! I could still walk. The palms of my hands were really burning now and were beginning to swell.

As I reached our front porch, tears welled up in my eyes. "Joe!" I limped as fast as I could to him. "I fell down! Look at my hands!"

The frightened look on his face was very satisfying. He took my hands and turned them palms up. "Poor, poor girl!" He hugged me and helped me to a chair.

It's been a week now, and I have an impressive bruise on my hip, and one of my hands is still a little swollen. All I have to do to get quick sympathy from Joe is frown or whimper as I move my wrists, or limp slightly and touch my hip.

Pride goes before destruction, a haughty spirit before a fall.

Proverbs 16:18

I didn't tell Joe that I was walking extra fast and looking at the sky. He might not sympathize with me anymore.

So, if you think you are standing firm, be careful that you don't fall.

1 Corinthians 10:12

Bedlam in the Baptistry

Joe is a deacon in our church, which fact somehow makes me a deaconess. We assist in communion and other worship-related services, and go to the deacons meetings once a month. In the past I have been assigned a few easy duties, such as bringing grape juice. A few months ago in the meeting we discussed what things would be like when our new sanctuary is finished.

"Right now," chairman Ray began, "when we have baptisms, we go to members' homes who have a pool, the candidates wear old clothes, and we use whatever towels are available. But in the new sanctuary, we'll have our own baptistry, and we'll need towels and robes." I nodded my head in approval.

"Who will volunteer to take care of buying towels?" Jan and Mary agreed they could handle that.

"Now we need volunteers to help in baptism. We need a deacon and a deaconess to give the candidates a towel when they come up out of the water."

I raised my hand. "Joe and I will be glad to do that, won't we, Hon'?" He didn't punch me, so it went down in the minutes that Joe and I would help in baptism.

After our first baptism in the new facility was scheduled, a member called me. "Mab, they tell me you're in charge of baptism."

"In charge? I thought I was only supposed to help."

As soon as we hung up, I called Ray. His wife told me that we were indeed in charge. We were to go to one of the churches in our denomination and borrow baptismal robes as well as find the new towels, hidden somewhere in the new kitchen.

Baptism Sunday arrived, and Joe and I were with Pastor Bob as he gave last-minute instructions to the candidates. When he finished, he pointed to us. "Just go with Joe and Mab. They'll take good care of you." That was probably the worst case of misplaced trust in his experience.

Because the church planners hadn't provided dressing rooms for the baptizees, we decided to put the women and girls in the library and the men and boys in a classroom.

In the new and empty library the women had no privacy. In the classroom where the men were dressing, the problem was that I'd given the biggest robes to the women. One fellow had to be dipped wearing his pants and shirt.

When the service began, the audience could see people come to the edge, then disappear. The baptistry was like a basement, and the water was deep, too. Fortunately, most people in California know how to swim. One big fellow slipped going in and fell against Pastor Bob, who is himself over six feet. Both almost went under the water without even a prayer.

As each person came up out of the water, we had intended to bestow a kiss on the cheek and say, "The

Lord be with you." But it was such a hassle to get them up the steps in those heavy, wet robes, we forgot about it. In fact, Joe and I were almost as wet as the candidates when we were through. It was appalling to see so much water slopped across the new carpets on the platform and halls and dripped into rooms. Thank heavens, the books hadn't been put in the library yet.

When it was over, Pastor Bob loped out and ran down the hall, a stream of water in his wake. I ran after him waving a towel, but he was in his study before I overtook him. "What a great day!" he grinned, grabbing the towel.

I have some recommendations to make at the next deacons' meeting. We need a lot more towels. We need our own robes. I suggest raincoats.

We need rubber treads on the baptistry steps and a crew standing by with mops. And we probably need somebody more efficient in charge of baptisms.

Then Jesus came from Galilee to the Jordan to be baptized by John.

Matthew 3:13

The next time Ray says he needs a volunteer, I'm going to pinch my mouth shut.

All of you who were baptized into Christ have clothed yourselves with Christ.

Galatians 3:27

Dictionary/ðik-ʃĕ-ner-ē

Working on homework, my grandson asked, "Grandmother, what does 'proletariat' mean?"

"Proletariat?" I looked up at the ceiling. Proletariat. I'd heard that word. Did it have something to do with protein? Production? "Well, David—" (I quit scraping carrots so that I could give him a superior look.) "I'll tell you what my mother—your great-grandmother—always told me. Go to the dictionary and look it up."

"You don't know what it means?"

"I didn't say that—but you won't learn anything if I *tell* you. Life isn't made up of easy answers."

"Guy!" he complained and slouched into the back bedroom where my desk and books are.

I finished the carrots and potatoes and added them to the roast, but he still was in my room. Drying my hands, I decided I'd better find him. He was seated at my desk, reading the dictionary. I put my hand on his shoulder. "Can't you find pro—pro—"

"Proletariat? Yeah, I found it. I've just been reading other words."

"The dictionary makes great reading." I grinned at him. "Except the stories are so short."

169

He ignored my joke. "Guess what 'prolix' means."

" 'Prolix'? Suppose you tell me."

"It's what the pastor is on Sunday mornings!" He guffawed, but I didn't get it. "Prolix means *long-winded!*"

I cleared my throat. "Of course."

"But you know what's weird about the illustrations? They always have pictures of things anybody knows—like snowshoes. They have this detailed drawing of snowshoes. And here's a picture of a sleigh—everybody knows what a sleigh is—and back here is a picture of a dog. Everybody in the world knows what a dog looks like. But there's no picture of an oppossum, or an orangutan, or a python, or a—"

"David, I think you better get back to your homework before your folks come for you. Tell me the meaning of pro—pro—"

"Proletariat? Means the lowest social or economic class in a community."

My eyebrows shot up in surprise. "Hmmm! That's right! Now, aren't you glad you looked it up?"

Humble yourselves before the Lord, and he will lift you up.

James 4:10

I felt a little guilty pretending I knew that word—but grandparents are supposed to know everything. Anyway, maybe sometime or other I did know what pro—that word meant.

Their tongue is a deadly arrow; it speaks with deceit.

Jeremiah 9:8

170

Hospital Halls

What a wild month this has been. Joe had open-heart surgery! I'm thankful to say that he is recovering faster and better than expected. I'm sure it's because so many were praying for him. Now, as I see him walking around, doing some of his chores, the fear and anxiety of those hospital days are a hazy memory. I can barely remember what CCU was like, or where his room was, or what I ate in the cafeteria. One thing, however, stands out clearly in my memory—the perplexing maze of those hospital halls.

An attendant showed us to Joe's room the first day. I was too worried and scared to remember where the elevators are, much less which way to turn when we stepped out. On the way down for his angiogram, Joe was on a gurney, so all I had to do was follow them down to the subterranean complex. After that and for the next ten days, I had to find my own way.

"He'll be in the cardiac care unit," the doctor said after the angiogram. "You can see him in about an hour." It was good he gave me an hour, because it took me almost that long to find CCU.

171

"Where's the elevator?" I finally blurted to a group of nurses, after dead-ending at Pediatrics.

"You go back down this hall, but then turn left and you'll see it."

On my first try I walked clear to the out-patient center before I realized I'd passed the left turn.

Getting out on the second floor, I walked down a hall that had many multiple choice intersections and very few signs. I walked for what seemed like a mile, but at last I came to a waiting room marked "CCU." Sinking down on a couch, I tried to remember. Had I turned left or right when I left the elevator? And how many other turns had I made?

That night, walking down dimmed halls, I almost despaired of ever finding the elevator, much less the parking lot. Besides, fate had another cruel trick in store. The elevator I boarded had doors on both ends, and naturally, the door that opened on the main floor led straight to Maternity.

The next day I determined not to be such a dumbbell. I read signs and tried to memorize the way, but when I left the elevator for CCU, I trudged down an identical hall to Geriatrics.

Finding the well-hidden cafeteria was a daily celebration. Then there would be the mystery of finding my way back up to Joe's room. These trips for food always hurt my self-esteem. Even a relatively easy trip to the restroom was fraught with dread after I turned left instead of right and entered the men's room.

On the last day, I found I wasn't alone in this corridor confusion. I was walking down the hall when a woman came toward me frowning, mumbling to herself, and looking up at signs. I knew immediately what her problem was. Lost! When we passed she gave me a tired smile. "Next time," she said, "I'll sprinkle bread crumbs so I can find my way."

For you were like sheep going astray, but now you have returned to the Shepherd and Overseer of your souls.

1 Peter 2:25

Joe and I decided to have lunch in the hospital cafeteria yesterday for "old time's sake." But he had to find it.

We all, like sheep, have gone astray.

Isaiah 53:6

Reunion with the Girls

Yesterday I went to a reunion luncheon with women I had known thirty years ago. I was excited and wanted to appear at my best. What should I wear that would make me seem youthful? What would hide my stomach? And should I wear big, long earrings and be in style, or wear tiny pearls and look demure and holy? Should I put a rinse on my hair to cover the gray? Should I use a foundation cream, or would the stuff get caught in my wrinkles and look worse?

I decided to wear my black and white dress and a black blazer, the most slenderizing thing in my wardrobe. I chose long earrings to show that I knew what is in style, yet short enough to be in good taste. I decided against a hair rinse but used just a little mascara on the gray hair around my face.

Then came the make-up. I put on my glasses and took a magnifying mirror over to the window to be sure that I didn't put on too much. Then I saw them. Long, white hairs hanging down in my eyebrows! Worse, black, stiff hairs on my upper lip and on my chin! Good grief. I was turning into a man. An old man. I got the tweezers and tried to pluck the stragglers in my eyebrows but couldn't reach them with my glasses on; and without them, even with the magnifying mirror, I couldn't see them. I closed my eyes and plucked where I thought they were in my eyebrows, upper lip, and chin. After several painful minutes I went on to an examination of the whole face. Magnified, it looked like a relief map of the Rocky Mountains. How could I have gotten so wrinkled in thirty years? When I had known "the girls," I had a flawless complexion, had rich brown hair, and 20-20 vision.

After parking, I took off my glasses and sort of groped my way into the restaurant where we were to meet. Three old women came toward me, smiling. One had snow-white hair, and the other two had liberal sprinklings of gray. I didn't know any of them, but could they possibly be some of "the girls?"

"I can't think of your name," the tallest said to me, "but I know you must be one of the old gang."

"And you're Phyllis," I said.

"No, I'm Fran."

"Oh, that's right! What's the matter with me! And you are—oh, what is your name?"

The rest of the women were already seated at a long table in one of the dining rooms.

At first I couldn't place anyone. I never saw so many old faces. Not many knew me, either, but gradually, the wrinkles, excess pounds, and white hair, were replaced by vibrant, youthful faces. I began to see each face as it had been so long ago. I'm sure the others were having the same experience, and before lunch was over we were the noisy, laughing bunch of women we used to be.

175

Again and again I could hear them say to each other, "You haven't changed at all!"

At home I looked at myself (not in the magnifying mirror). My eyes were sparkley—as well as I could see without my glasses—and compared to them, I guess I didn't look any worse or any better. I don't know why I had bothered to endure the pain of pulling out those hairs. "The girls" probably couldn't have seen them. Most of them hadn't worn their glasses, either.

Gray hair is a crown of splendor.
Proverbs 16:31

I don't know why I don't just let down and get old—I can't be glamorous forever!

Likewise, teach the older women to be reverent in the way they live. . . . Then they can train the younger women . . . so that no one will malign the word of God.
Titus 2:3–5

Exercise

Since Joe had his open-heart surgery, we have become more aware of diet and exercise than ever before. "Fat, too much salt, and lack of exercise is what brought this on," Joe's doctor told us. "And the new artery replacements will clog up even faster. You have to change your life-style."

Joe goes to cardiac rehabilitation three times a week, where he walks a treadmill, rides a stationary bike, and uses a rowing machine. On the mornings he is gone, I turn on a TV aerobics program and do what they do—sort of. On alternate days we walk two miles together. I don't know which exercise I hate the most. A friend told me that her first thought in the morning is of the Lord. I know that's how it should be, but my first thought is, "Rats! Exercise!"

The loud, jazzy music helps me do aerobics, but the women on that show are so physically fit that I feel hopeless. They're slender, yet have curves in the right places, shown off by skintight outfits. While they are doing jumping jacks a foot high, they keep smiling or talking, not the least out of breath. Just as I decide to rest a moment, the leader calls, "Don't sit down! Come on! You're doing fine." So I struggle on, trying to do "grasshoppers," "flea hops," and "Freddies." One day they announced they would be using a jump rope, and to go get one before the routines began. I ran out to the garage and found a piece of rope we had used for a leash when we took care of somebody's dog. On the first try I tripped and lurched toward Samson, who always sits watching my antics, with somber turquoise eyes. When he saw me falling toward him, he leaped sideways, cracking his head on the coffee table. Poor guy. I didn't see him again until afternoon. After a couple more false starts, I sort of got the hang of it. The rope kept hitting the ceiling, and little bits of acoustic tile fell on the carpet. When I was out of breath and had to quit, it looked like a mini-hailstorm had passed through. I admit, though, *after* the half hour is over and my heart rate returns to normal, I feel good.

When Joe and I walk, I try to keep my mind off my aching joints by looking at the houses, trees, and flowers. I pick up things on our walks—seed pods, pretty leaves, a black feather. One day I found a dime. All these things help pass the time until our two-mile walk is done. When I get tired, I take a deep breath and say, "Come on arteries! Open up and let the blood through. Make some new veins because I am going to keep exercising until the Lord comes, and you might as well get used to it."

Tomorrow is aerobics day, but I just heard on the news that they have discovered that high-impact aerobics has caused light-headedness and ringing of the ears in some people! Maybe I'll just work in the flower beds tomorrow. That should be exercise enough.

Therefore do not worry about tomorrow, for tomorrow will worry about itself. Each day has enough trouble of its own.

Matthew 6:34

I can't help thinking about my mother-in-law. Ninety-one, eats whatever she wants, pours on the salt, drinks coffee, never exercises, yet is in perfect health. How come?

Do you not know that your body is a temple of the Holy Spirit ... you were bought at a price. Therefore honor God with your body.

1 Corinthians 6:19–20

Chef

I often wonder why some women love to cook. How could anyone *love* to cook? When I'm with a group of women and they talk about a marvelous recipe for chicken, or a new pie filling, I feel so inadequate. I never have anything to say about my recipes because usually anything new I try is either runny or burned. Why couldn't I have been born with a flair for cooking gourmet meals, or at least the ability to make a decent casserole? My mother was a good cook. All my female relatives are good cooks, but as soon as I walk in the kitchen I get a stress attack. Is something missing from my genes?

In the past it didn't matter so much. When the kids were home, I was careful to have the four basic foods— meat, vegetables, starch, and fruit—I think those are the basics. Anyway, we ate hamburgers and hot dogs (meat), french fries and canned corn (vegetables), apples and oranges (fruits). We had plenty of doughnuts, cookies, and cake (starches). We had our dairy products, too— whole milk and ice cream.

After the kids left home, Joe and I began to eat out

more often. I love to eat out, whether it's a hamburger or a fancy meal. Now, since Joe's surgery, all that is changed. We both have to watch our blood pressure and cholesterol. Gone are the happy hamburger days, the Mexican food, doughnuts, candy bars, and Danish. Because I want us to live longer, I am forced to cook right. Every bit of meat now has to be "THREE-B'd"— baked, broiled, or boiled. Have you tried boiled hamburger lately? We are not to eat red meat more than twice a week, and only six ounces per day. A six-ounce steak for Joe is two bites.

We're not supposed to use canned goods anymore— too much salt. I prepare our vegetables now, never having realized before how dangerous that can be. I cut my thumb last week peeling beets, and my knuckles are raw from grating carrots. A couple of days ago I made soup with beef stock, fresh vegetables, and noodles. No salt. Joe said, "This needs spices or something, Babe. I can't eat it." The next day I heated it up and added a bit of cinnamon and cloves, but he still wouldn't eat it. When I poured it down the sink, even the garbage disposal growled.

We're supposed to eat fish at least three times a week. Just the thought of that big-mouthed trout I baked, with its eyes glaring at me, makes me sick. But they say that fish helps you live longer, so this week I'm going to try boiling cod with some garlic. And yet, the thought keeps running around in my mind—*why do I want to live longer if I have to eat my cooking?*

The Israelites started wailing... "If only we had meat to eat ... we never see anything but this manna!"

Numbers 11:4, 6

Maybe I should ask the prayer chain to pray that our cholesterol will come down.

Do not crave his delicacies, for that food is deceptive.

Proverbs 23:3

Pardon Me?

I feel a little grumpy this morning. I've about decided I need a hearing aid. For over a year now I've had to ask Joe every night to turn up the TV so I can hear it. I can live with that, but what I hate is when I'm with other people and I can't hear what they're saying. If only they'd quit mumbling!

We went out to dinner last night with Joan and Don, and Pastor Bob and Barbara. Don is so clever with "one-liners," but while they were laughing at his quips, I was trying to figure out what he said. Pastor Bob told a funny story about their first church and at the end everyone roared, but I didn't hear the punch line. Besides missing the jokes, I had a hard time trying to follow the conversation. For a while I thought they were talking about the pioneers, and then Don said "I've read a lot about German pastry."

"German pastry?" I whispered to Joe.

"*Mormon history, Babe.*"

It's hard for me to understand Barbara even face-to-face because she speaks softly and has a Southern accent. Last night she was seated across the table, yet I could only hear about every third word. I saw her mouth moving, and she was looking right at me, but her words sounded like, "How're your fun and lotto ball doing in their chemistry?"

I blinked. "Pardon me?"

She cleared her throat and spoke loudly. "Ah said, 'how're your son and daughta-in-law doin' in their ministry?'" Oh. She didn't have to shout.

Bob was telling us something about his car being trouble, and I got all pop-eyed because I thought he said something about a scar being double.

It's harder to hear in restaurants, but that isn't the only place I struggle. We were at the hospital last week because one of our friends was having an angiogram. When the doctor came out, we gathered around him. "I want her to have an Italian treadmill test in the next week or so."

On the way home I said to Joe, "I wonder what an Italian treadmill test is."

Joe shook his head. "Not *Italian*. Thalium! It's a dye that will show what her arteries are doing on the treadmill test."

Maybe I can learn to lip-read.

For the eyes of the Lord are on the righteous and his ears are attentive to their prayer.

1 Peter 3:12

Getting deaf isn't fun. On the other hand, it's nice not to hear the dogs barking at night, or Larita's rooster crowing in the morning.

No ear has heard what God has prepared for those who love him.

1 Corinthians 2:9

Bug Off, Oven Off!

It's sort of a tradition with me to do my once-a-year oven cleaning job after Thanksgiving and before Christmas. Cooking a turkey dinner makes such a mess. Grease spatters all over and burns, chunks of dressing fall out and burn, and drips from sweet potatoes and pumpkin pie are even worse. In fact, by the time Thanksgiving Day is over I can't even heat up leftovers in the oven without filling the house with a foul-smelling smoke. The next day, after all the dishes and silver are put away, I wipe off the burners and the outside of the oven; thus, no one can even know what a mess is inside. But I can't cook anything in it until I can scrounge up the courage to clean it.

And it does take courage. Just reading the directions on the oven cleaners is enough to scare me. "Wear rubber gloves to protect hands. Protect floor. Do not spray in face. Do not breathe spray mist. Do not spray on exterior surfaces. Do not spray pilot light. Keep off all electrical connections. DANGER. KEEP OUT OF REACH OF CHILDREN." And the first-aid directions aren't much comfort, either. Evidently, this stuff can literally dissolve a person to death if she doesn't get immediate medical attention.

185

In spite of the danger and because it has been four days since Thanksgiving, I decided this morning I'd better get at it. After I had spread newspapers on the floor, donned rubber gloves, and tied one of Joe's handkerchiefs on my face, I opened the oven. It looked like a charcoal broiler after a hamburger fry. The once-shiny chrome racks were burned black, chunks of burned dressing had turned to gray clinkers. Burned syrup from the pies had made pools of black shellac. I scraped out what I could, then picked up the can of oven cleaner and sprayed everything inside for as long as I could hold my breath. Slamming the oven door, I ran outside, took deep gasps of fresh air, and waited a half hour for it to do its stuff.

As soon as I inserted one rubber-gloved hand into that slimy brown yuk, my nose began to itch with the fury of a mosquito bite. At the same time my head began to itch. Hopefully, I've developed an allergic reaction to cleaning the oven and in the future can give that job to Joe. In spite of the maddening itching, I tried to follow the over-simplified instructions: "Simply wipe clean with a cloth or sponge." I wiped, sponged, scrubbed, and grumbled for at least two hours and changed the hot, soapy water in the sink at least four times. At last, the oven was shiny and clean again.

Now all I have to do is convince some other members of the family to have Christmas at their house— or, if they want to come here, let it be a carry-in affair. I'm not about to cook *anything* in my oven the rest of the year.

. . . like whitewashed tombs, which look beautiful on the outside but on the inside are full of dead men's bones and everything unclean.

Matthew 23:27

Actually, I don't know why I bother to clean the oven. It will just get dirty again, and nobody sees it but me.

The Lord does not look at the things man looks at. Man looks at the outward appearance, but the Lord looks at the heart.

1 Samuel 16:7

Christmas Blues

"It's only the fifth of December," I said to Joan over the phone, "and we're already getting Christmas cards!"

"I know! I haven't even bought mine yet!"

"How can people be so efficient? And every year we get cards from people we don't know—like this one—the Pelegars—Judith, Chris, Tommy, and Step. Did we ever know any Pelegars?"

"Not that I remember—but that's not saying much. I can barely remember the kids' names in my class. Where do they live?"

"No return. And this one: 'Love, The Wilsons. Looking forward to seeing you in the new year.'"

"Mother, you must know them!"

"I've wracked my brain, but maybe I can't remember because I'm worried about Christmas shopping. Do you have any idea what we can buy for Mom? She's got everything."

"How about body powder, or perfume?"

"Good idea! I'll give her that awful LeClinche Parfum I got last Christmas."

"Mother! *I* gave you that!"

"Oooh . . . I'm sorry—but honestly, Honey, it smells like fly spray."

"Why do we have to give presents anyway?" Joan sounded sad. "We usually buy something the person doesn't want—"

"That's true," I agreed.

"Or you buy something for someone who doesn't give you anything, or vice versa—then you both feel bad. Anyway, the reason I called—what do you want me to bring for Christmas?"

"I don't know. I'm tired of turkey, and ham is too salty. How about picking up forty hamburgers at McDonald's?"

"Be serious, Mother. Hosting Christmas dinner for fifteen is scary, and I want to help."

"I love Christmas, but it *is* hard. I read the other day that it's the most stressful time of the year."

"I believe it," Joan said. "Addressing all the cards, extra shopping, baking, decorating the tree, gift wrapping—"

"And the men don't do very much, either!"

"Exactly! If it weren't for women, there probably wouldn't be much Christmas celebration."

We were suddenly silent. I don't know what she was thinking, but I was wondering, *What insane force takes hold of women that makes them shop, bake, wrap, cook, hurry, and worry most of December? Why?*

"Glory to God in the highest, and on earth peace."

Luke 2:14

189

I wonder what would happen if women in America would band together and boycott Christmas craziness and simply worship Him on His birthday?

He will be called Wonderful Counselor, Mighty God, Everlasting Father, Prince of Peace.

Isaiah 9:6

No Room

It was dark, everyone had gone home, and I was trying to get the courage to clean up the kitchen. The girls had done a lot—washed dishes twice and carried out all the gift wrappings—but the food was still all over and had to be consolidated and put away.

Joe followed me out to the kitchen and made a turkey sandwich. "Well, what did you think of the kitchen? Was it roomier than last year?"

I looked around. Every inch of the new counter space on both sides of the sink was covered. There were plates with one or two cookies left on them, bowls with a few chips in the bottom, the turkey platter, a basket with one roll peeking out from under the napkin, three pie plates with a piece or two in each, paper plates, and napkins. Both sinks were full of dishes and utensils. The stove top was covered with pans, and my beautiful floor was a collage of jello blurbs, cookie crumbs, a gravy spill—even a piece of turkey the cats had missed.

I scowled at Joe. "This is probably not the best time to ask me about the virtues of the kitchen." He looked so sad I immediately tried to make amends. "But, really, it is much, much better than last Christmas."

He didn't look convinced. "I'm sorry I'm not a rich man so that you could have a fine home to entertain in."

"Oh, Joe! Remember last year I had the card table up in that corner and two TV trays over there, and there wasn't enough space for things?"

"You still don't have enough space when we have the whole family." He compressed his lips and frowned. "I wonder if I could—"

"Honey, it's fine! Really it is."

He went to the back porch and looked all around. My heart began to thud. (That's how he looks just before he starts knocking out a partition.) "Honey—please—what are you thinking?"

"Oh—just that if I take out this wall, move the washer and dryer out to the patio, I could extend the counter by five feet."

"I have a better idea," I said. "I'll just tell Joan and Barbara that Christmas is going to be at one of their houses next year."

But if we have food and clothing, we will be content with that.

1 Timothy 6:8

I'll bet if I had a kitchen twice this size, I'd still have it cluttered to the max.

I consider that our present sufferings are not worth comparing with the glory that will be revealed in us.

Romans 8:18

192

Gift Exchange

When we came back from the mall, our neighbor, Larita, and her puppy, Gismo, were walking by. "Where have you been?" she asked.

"Oh, exchanging defective Christmas presents," I answered.

"I know what you mean. I bought a watch and it wouldn't run. When I took it back, they didn't have any more like it."

"Joe bought me a vegetable dish to match the new dishes Ron and Barb gave me, but it had a big blemish in it."

Gismo looked up at me with mournful eyes.

"Another gift," I continued, "was a bottle of Oscar de la Renta perfume, but when I opened the package an eighth of it was gone. It was leaking all over the package."

"That stuff is expensive."

"The clerk said it happens all the time. Can you believe it?"

"Yeah, I believe it."

"Then Joan and Don gave us a Toastmaster oven, but

when we tried to make toast the button wouldn't stay down. The poor woman in home appliances didn't even question us. She just pointed to a stack of new ones and said, 'Take your pick.'"

That night, while Joe was trying to get a new portable phone to work, I decided to mend his socks. I despise mending, but he had been so patient while we exchanged stuff at the mall, and this was a favorite pair.

"You know, Honey," I said, with a light bulb in his sock, needle poised over the hole. "I just can't get over the poor workmanship in merchandise today. Think of all the things we had to exchange—"

"We may have to take this cotton-pickin' phone back if I can't get it to work."

"—and other people are going through it, too. Larita said she had to take back a watch. Why do people put out such shoddy work?"

He glanced over at what I was doing. "Well—I don't know. People don't have pride in their work anymore. By the way—" He paused, and I looked over at him. "Thank you for mending my socks."

"You're welcome." I smiled at him, pleased that he noticed how noble I was.

"I just wonder, though—"

"Yes?"

His blue eyes twinkled. "Why are you using green thread on black socks?"

Whatever your hand finds to do, do it with all your might.

Ecclesiastes 9:10

194

*What difference does it make if the thread is green or black?
Nobody can see it inside his shoe.*

Whatever you do, do it all for the glory of God.
1 Corinthians 10:31

Older, Maybe

I sighed with relief as I put the last sack of New Year's groceries in the trunk and slammed the lid. Oh no! Not again! I went back in the market and called Joe.

When he drove up in his pickup, he was shaking his head and grinning. As he unlocked the trunk, he said, "You must be getting old, Babe. This is the second time this month."

"Young people get locked out, too," I pouted.

"True." He handed me my keys. "But you are forgetful. How about forgetting to enter the insurance payment on the check record?"

I stamped my foot. "That doesn't make me old! I've always done things like that."

"Tell me about it!" He kissed my cheek, and as he drove away he called, "Maybe you'd better buy some Geritol!"

Gr-r-r! He could make me so mad. I know I'm getting older. But I'm not old. Am I? The kids have teased me about forgetting things, and I hate it when they look at each other when I can't remember something *they* say

196

they told me. I think they forget to *tell me* what they claim they said.

In the New Year I've got to prove I'm not old. I don't usually make resolutions, but I think I'm going to do a few things this year to show my family I'm still young. At heart, anyway.

For one thing, I think I'll buy a pair of roller blades like Judi's. Maybe I'd better check my health insurance first, but what could be more youthful than skimming along with my hair blowing in the breeze? My hair is too short to blow very far, but maybe I'll let it grow. And then I'm going to learn how to break-dance. I'll probably need to find a chiropractor, but wouldn't my moves wow the kids?

I think I'll buy some earrings at least five inches long, and get some metallic pants that fasten around the ankles. I'd better get some four-inch heels to wear with them, too.

Good-bye to all my double-knit slacks. From now on I'm only going to buy trendy, wrinkled clothes—the wilder the colors, the better!

Of course, if I do all the above, my family will know I'm old and in my second childhood.

When I drove in the garage, Joe came out to help me bring in the groceries. I looked up at him piteously. "Do you really think I'm old?"

"Why sure, Honey. We both are."

"That's too sad! Why do we have to get old?"

"It's God's way. Have you considered the alternative?" He hugged me. "It's not that bad, Babe. I still love you, even if you forget. I even love your wrinkles!"

Praise the Lord, O my soul . . . who satisfies [my] desires with good things, so that [my] youth is renewed like the eagle's.

Psalm 103:1, 5

My mirror tells me I'm not getting old — I am old. But that's just my skin. My inside self is still enjoying life.

Forgetting what is behind and straining toward what is ahead, I press on toward the goal to win the prize for which God has called me heavenward in Christ Jesus.

Philippians 3:13–14

198